RICHES
— OF —
GLORY

LARRY THOMPSON

SECRETS OF THE KINGDOM SERIES

STREAMS OF GLORY
m i n i s t r i e s

FOREWORD

Jesus had just found out His friend Lazarus was sick and purposely waited two more days before responding to the call by Lazarus's sisters to come and heal him. He waited so that Lazarus would surely die before He got there and the glory of God could be revealed in Him, proving that God sent Him and that He was the resurrection and the life. People would place their trust in Jesus, and the Father would receive glory through Him.

Jesus said He was going to wake Lazarus up because he was asleep. Waking from sleep for a believer is a metaphor for rising from the dead to a new life. That is for someone who goes to sleep having put their faith in Christ. Only those who die "in Christ" get to participate in this new creation life.

Those who have this new life also have a light residing within them that the rest of the world does not have. It's a transforming and informing light. This light is the glory of Father for anyone who is positioned "in Christ". This "in Christ" position gives us the power of the Throne of Glory, because we are sons of glory.

But as many as received Him, to them He gave the right to become children of God, to those who believe in His name: (John 1:12)

In Him was life, and the life was the light of men. (John 1:4)

But God, who is rich in mercy, because of His great love with which He loved us, even when we were dead in trespasses, made us alive together with Christ (by grace you have been saved), and raised us up together, and made us sit together in the heavenly places in Christ Jesus, that in the ages to come He might show the exceeding riches of His grace in His kindness toward us in Christ Jesus. (Ephesians 2:4-7)

Therefore, if anyone is in Christ, he is a new creation; old things have passed away; behold, all things have become new. (2 Corinthians 5:17)

This transforming "light" is the glory of the Father which resides within each of us upon putting our faith in Christ, but it lies dormant (we are blind to it even as believers) until we know that it is in us. When we know...our eyes begin to open and we can see from within in a way the world cannot see. We know things we are not supposed to know from the world's perspective. Yet we are supposed to know them from the Father's perspective.

Sometimes God waits until we think the worst has happened and there's no turning back before He sends His answer by telling us He can turn it back, so that His full glory will be revealed in any given situation. Do not ever think death (or sleep) is the end of anything. God will wake that person up if you trust in Him to do so and cause all who witness to believe in Him. Nothing is impossible for our God and for those who are in Christ.

Jesus said to the disciples, "Let us go to Judea again."

The disciples said to Him, "Rabbi, lately the Jews sought to stone You, and are You going there again?"

Jesus answered, "Are there not twelve hours in the day? If anyone walks in the day, he does not stumble, because he sees the light of this world. But if one walks in the night, he stumbles, because the light is not in him." (John 11:8-10)

"Because the light is not in him"—that is why he stumbles—not because it is dark outside. But because he's spiritually blind. There's no light in him. When a Christian stumbles it is because no light is in him, same as the world. Sight is not automatic even upon putting our trust in Christ. God's glory must be awakened from lying dormant within us. The potential for sight is always there. But our eyes still must be opened. So the Holy Spirit is teaching us all things.

Awake, O sleeper, arise from the dead, and Christ will shine on you. (Ephesians 5:14 ESV)

Jesus' disciples did not want to go back to Judea because they did not want to die along with Lazarus (hence Thomas' sarcastic comment in John 11:16). The Jews had just recently tried to stone Jesus there. But Jesus was not worried because He could see perfectly all the way to the end of God's glory being revealed when Lazarus would rise from the dead. He was called to go to Lazarus by the Father and nothing could stop that from taking place. Jesus did not need to know everything He would encounter along the way, although He probably did know beforehand. He only needed to see God's glory being revealed at the end of it all. Jesus could see by the light of the glory, which is the Father who was always with Him.

The Father is what made Jesus the light of the world as long as He was in the world. Jesus gave us this same light to walk in as long as we are in the world, because He gave us the Father's glory, the same glory Jesus had before the world was. Jesus restored us to our Father by making us One in Him (in Christ).

I am the light of the world. He who follows Me shall not walk in darkness, but have the light of life. (John 8:12)

Awake, my glory!
Awake, lute and harp!
I will awaken the dawn. (Psalm 57:8)

And now, O Father, glorify Me together with Yourself, with the glory which I had with You before the world was...And the glory which You gave Me I have given them, that they may be one just as We are one: I in them, and You in Me; that they may be made perfect in one, and that the world may know that You have sent Me, and have loved them as You have loved Me. (John 17:5, 22-23)

∞∞∞∞

When I first met Larry Thompson, the author (co-author to the Spirit of Glory), the Father had already been drawing me to Himself; as He is with anyone who has decided to read this book. At the time, I had already known Jesus on an increasing level for the better part of 21 years and I loved Him dearly. I also knew the Father to a certain degree, and called Him "Papa". The revelation of the *kingdom of heaven* had just been revealed to me and I had that "Aha!" moment when I fully realized that heaven was *in me*. This caused a giant paradigm shift in my thinking and perspective: heaven was looking out through my eyes at everything around me, and I belonged to heaven—it is my home. However, I did not yet have this "knowledge of the glory", as Larry is so richly saturated in. He has a 16 year lead time on most of us, so he is the lead-runner in the field on this topic of the glory. Yet this truth: the Good News of the Father's glory came into my life immediately following the revelation of the kingdom of heaven within me. I understand now, after almost two years has passed, that the glory of the Father saturates the atmosphere of His kingdom, so that once we enter in through that Door of Christ, we immediately breathe Him in —the Father of glory!—and everything changes in our lives (and minds) at an exponential rate.

According to 2 Thessalonians 2:14, the purpose of the Gospel, which called us, is for the *obtaining of the glory* of our Lord Jesus Christ. This simply means Jesus *restored us to the Father* in Himself, making us sons of the same glory, and joint-heirs with Christ. Christ is the access Door for us into the Father's Presence. Jesus did all that He did, including ascending to the Father, in order to lock us permanently in place—in the Father—much like an aircraft that is getting refueled in flight, only it is a permanent *locking in*—restored! Reconciled to the Father! In this way, we obtain all the *Riches of Glory* through inheritance as true sons and daughters of our Father who is in heaven.

I am convinced that, other than the Bible, this is the most anointed, powerful, revelatory, enlightening, transformative, and prophetic book you will have ever read to date. You will not be the same person at the end of the book as you are at the beginning, and there is no going back once you read it, but you will not ever want to go back. There is absolutely no prophetic voice out there anywhere that is higher than the knowledge of the glory of our Father, which is given to us by being positioned in Christ. Jesus agrees with me, or rather, I agree with Him.

You have heard Me say to you, 'I am going away and coming *back* to you.' If you loved Me, you would rejoice because I said, 'I am going to the Father,' for My Father is greater than I. (John 14:28)

We did not earn this privilege to live in the Father's Presence; to have His unconditional love; to know He loves us in the same way He loves Jesus. The Father is the one Who qualified us and drew us to Himself, simply because He truly does love us no matter what we have had to go through to get to where we are now.

Father, bless all who begin this journey of being restored permanently to You in Christ, who will inherit all the *Riches of Glory*. Whatever they are suffering right now, give them the revelation on Romans 8:18; that their suffering was meant for Your glory, and that glory is SOON to be revealed in them. Every negative condition that Your Son, Jesus, faced on earth, living as a Man under the Old Covenant, walking in Old Covenant glory, He transformed into glory. And the glory of the New Covenant is much greater than the glory of the Old. Father, ignite the imaginations of the ones reading this, and give them the heart of a child to believe Your Word that all things truly are possible in Christ. Father, please give them Your wisdom and favor as You pour in revelation of who You are to them, and who they are to You, so they can learn to fully cooperate with the Holy Spirit: to hear His voice; to say only what they hear Him saying, and to do only what they see Him doing. Father, also give them perfect peace as they keep their minds on You, because they are learning to trust in You; and give them perfect love that casts out all fear. Thank You Father for Your generous heart toward us. To You be all the glory for what You are about to do in their lives! In Jesus Name, Yes and Amen.

Rodna M. Epley
Biblical Leadership
Southwestern Christian University, Bethany

CONTENTS

Riches of Glory

1

Crown Jewel of Heaven

*D*uring the summer of 2000, my kids and I went camping in the Three Sisters Wilderness area located in the Cascade Range within the Willamette and Deschutes National Forests in Oregon. I had given much thought into planning the trip for several weeks leading up to it. It has always been refreshing just to get away from the sounds of the city. To enter this natural setting with trees, mountains and streams in all of its serenity and majestic beauty is a joy—and a privilege. As the psalmist wrote, "Be still, and know that I am God..." (Psalm 46:10 NKJV). The sound of the wind as it stirs the branches of the pine trees, the cool breeze upon our faces, and the fresh scent of mountain air heightens all senses. These are the kind of experiences that God intended for us to enjoy with Him.

These outdoor encounters with God have had the greatest impact on my soul. The whole experience is very calming. It creates sensitivity to His Spirit and an awareness that everything is coming together, as life begins to make sense. What is my part in this vastness? How do I fit in with the Father's plan? It is during these quiet times that one can reflect upon what is most important. Following the Holy Spirit into these wilderness adventures makes it that much more rewarding with all that He reveals. Most of the distractions which capture my attention and interests are set aside, so that I can enjoy time with the Father and His creation as He pervades the very core of my being.

Now I was delighted to be sharing this joyful time with my children. The contemplation put forth into this outing included a unique surprise in store for them. They had never been to this particular area and would not have known beforehand what I already knew. I often did spontaneous things; however, on this particular adventure I had imagined in advance what the kids might enjoy, and I chose to catch them unexpectedly in complete amazement. It had always been my heart's desire to have many experiences like this one with my children, enjoying each day as if it were the very last. I wanted to create memories that would be cherished years later when reflecting upon times we had enjoyed together as a family.

We set up our camp and gathered wood right away so that when evening came we could enjoy sitting around the campfire. We roasted hotdogs and made s'mores—a necessity for any camper. Although it is amusing now to think that I had never heard of s'mores until after I had been born-again. The first time I was introduced to these campfire treats had been at a youth outing where someone cried out,

"We are having s'mores!" I had no idea what s'mores were, but the description was quickly volunteered, "They are so good that you just want *s'more*!" It can be surprising to realize the many things in life we take for granted. I have encountered many people with different backgrounds who haven't had the opportunity to experience what my family has enjoyed as a norm; yet, they do not have the understanding of certain concepts or the rich images that have developed in me from these memories with my children.

Another unique example that contributed to building important concepts was during a visit I made to the Ukraine. I promised some people from a translator service that if they could find an apartment for me with an oven, I would make them pizza. They found an apartment for me, and I made them pizza. Before I left that area of the country, the Ukrainian translators gave me a going-away party. While discussing many different topics, one of the translators who had eaten my pizza asked me how I made it. I answered, "That was a million-dollar formula." This put a value on my recipe, which I only intended to share with those who were family and close friends; however, I did offer one step in the process, "I can tell you how I *bake* it. I let it bake 'til it is a *marshmallow toast brown*." I was referring to how campers might prepare marshmallows for s'mores. Their response took me by surprise, "What are marshmallows?" They had never heard of *marshmallows*. How do you describe something which seems so simple to someone who has never seen or heard of it before?

The next morning from our camp (in Oregon), my children and I set out to go hiking to explore places up on the Tam McArthur Rim. A long trail meanders to the top where you need to be sure-footed because of all the loose rocks and uneven ground. I held my youngest one's hand most of the way up and back down the trail. I had been hiking in this vicinity one August a few years prior and stood on the snow-covered mountain wearing shorts; a friend took a picture of that moment. I was hoping during this trip to discover that the winter snow at the higher elevations would still have large patches available to enjoy.

That evening we made lunches and packed them in our backpacks so that we would be prepared for a much longer hike the next day. Candice decided not to go hiking with us up the mountainside a second time and stayed behind with her grandma for the day. It was more than she wanted to contend with. The other three kids went with me expecting another day of exploring the mountains. When we reached the point from the day before, where I had discovered that snow was indeed still on the hillside, my children expressed to me, "It would be fun to go sledding in the snow during the summertime!" Little did they know, *sledding* was the surprise I had in mind for them. I had taken the liberty of placing in their packs a deflated inner tube along with an air canister and hand pump. They had hiked most of the morning without ever discovering what I deposited in their packs.

This is exactly what the Heavenly Father has done with us. We do not know all that He deposited inside of us when He deposited His glory—the crown jewel of heaven! "She will place on your head an ornament of grace; a crown of glory she will deliver to you" (Proverbs 4:9 NKJV). That *she* is the personification of wisdom. Jesus has become our wisdom.

We all took turns filling the inner-tube with air from the hand pump after the air canister had been emptied. Now we were ready to slide down the hill. This was thrilling for them, having fun in the sun and inner-tubing in shorts! It was just as much a thrill for me to anticipate this moment, to know how they might react, and to enjoy what had been planned in advance. I truly believe that this had been inspired within me by the Holy Spirit. We follow Him through love, while Love directs our thoughts and how we make decisions. "In this the love of God was manifested toward us, that God has sent His only begotten Son into the world, that we might live through Him" (1 John 4:9 NKJV).

After about an hour of sliding, we continued our trek up to higher ground, almost to the 8,000 feet level. We sat and ate our lunches together while viewing the whole panorama, looking at the distant peaks, and enjoying the breathtaking scenery that our God had made. We stood apart on the heights of this Cascade Range. We had conquered the mountain and enjoyed what very few people (if any) would have done during the summertime. I took a photo of my crew, capturing this moment with the backdrop of that final jagged peak of Broken Top. This experience is one that would be remembered for a long time to come.

The understanding of the *knowledge of the glory* is pre-eminent on the Father's heart and mind. He has deposited within us His *glory*. We had no idea what was in His thoughts or what He had planned for us. How would we have known this, and why is that so important to the believer? When we remember that Jesus only spoke what He heard the Father saying, we receive greater insight from the heart of the Father as it is being expressed through the words Jesus expressed in prayer.

Father, I desire that they also whom You gave Me may be with Me where I am, that they may behold My glory which You have given Me; for You loved Me before the foundation of the world (John 17:24 NKJV).

2

Dimensions of Glory

*T*here are different dimensions of His glory, which are profound in every way. We will never exhaust all the possibilities that are placed before us by the Holy Spirit. For those that are mentioned in the book of Ephesians, chapter three, I will identify the significance of how all the promises from the Father are manifested in the different dimensions that He has placed in Scripture.

For this reason I bow my knees to the Father of our Lord Jesus Christ, from whom the whole family in heaven and earth is named, that He would grant you, according to the riches of His glory, to be strengthened with might through His Spirit in the inner man, that Christ may dwell in your hearts through faith; that you, being rooted and grounded in love, may be able to comprehend with all the saints what is the **width** and **length** and **depth** and **height**—to know the love of Christ which passes knowledge; that you may be filled with all the fullness of God. (Ephesians 3:14–19 NKJV)

When a Scripture promise leaps off the page at us because of how it is impacting our heart and thoughts, then the depth of wisdom from the Holy Spirit is beginning to be unleashed in that exact verse. When that happens, it is a good time to begin praying with joy, knowing within us that we already have the victory. It is not this way: that we are *going* to get victory. It is accurately stated in Scripture that we already *have* the victory. Jesus sees the end from the beginning. He sees in that spiritual realm the end or outcome of something right from the start. He sees the *victory* at the onset of any confrontation and struggle. He sent His Holy Spirit to teach and train our spiritual eyes to see things in the same way. The practical means for accomplishing this is through unveiling the hidden wisdom from any promise. That promise has become a *living* promise instead of a black and white written promise.

"Let the weak say, 'I am strong.'" (Joel 3:10 NKJV) In this promise, the weak are saying they are strong while they are weak. What is taking place in the spiritual realm, called His *glory*, is the power and authority in His *promise* that is being released by us through our spoken words. The glory is the very substance that transforms the condition. The Father's glory permeates our words. "And since we have the same spirit of faith, according to what is written, 'I believed and therefore I spoke,' we also believe and therefore speak" (2 Corinthians 4:13 NKJV).

Remaining in Christ—remaining in the Light—is that steady stream of His glory which purges all our thoughts so that they align with His thoughts. This purging transforms our minds. We still have this residue of the old nature in us, but we have His Holy Spirit putting to death that old nature through a willing heart to work with Him. The resistance we face more than anything else is our own pride which is at the seat of the old nature. The new nature is the new creation and it is flooded with His love. The two natures do not merge. Though we are aware of this old residue within us, we still surrender ourselves continually as we surrender to Him in communion.

That yielded state of mind—that surrendered heart— puts to death the old nature. The struggle is fierce and even becomes darkest before the dawn, but His light becomes brighter than the noon sun. This light is not only the brightness of His glory, but also it is His wisdom and power that streams through us. The experiences in Him are the result of our ability to say *yes* and *amen* (2 Corinthians 1:20). Those two keys are the access to every promise He has given. We have not yet experienced all that could be known by any one promise, for the very nature of all His promises is eternal. We enter in and receive then partake of His divine nature through our knowledge of Him and by appropriating His promises in our lives (2 Peter 1:3–4).

Thanks be to God who has sent His Holy Spirit. The very private lessons and tutoring from the Holy Spirit, who teaches and guides our lives, are very simple and practical for operating in His glory beyond all that we could possibly think, ask, or imagine (Ephesians 3:20–21). This personal, very intimate training by the Holy Spirit accurately aligns all of our thoughts, desires, and dreams so that they become permeated with His divine nature. We are *one* by what *He* does in our lives, not by what *we* do. We only follow His leading, direction, and voice, which puts us on course with the exact purposes of the Father. That is the sum totality of how important it is to follow and obey the voice of the Holy Spirit—intimately from a heart that is yielded to Him.

Acquiescence is such a word that describes the character and temperament of a true disciple, and will identify the kind of heart God is transforming us into by being in Christ. It has this full meaning: perfect, peaceful, submissive, and surrender. When we take on the nature of the Holy Spirit in our lives, it becomes perfect, complete in Him. His peace radiates within us and directs us, even in all our prayers. It guards our hearts and minds. We learn how to submit ourselves one to another. We are surrendered to His Word and purposes in our lives. The very life and glory of Jesus permeates our whole being. "For in Him we live and move and have our being, as also some of your own poets have said, 'For we are also His offspring'" (Acts 17:28 NKJV).

This is a refining word over things He has already been speaking to us, and it is being refined more and more all the time. We listen to the voice of the Holy Spirit, which is everything. Many will say we have to obey (and we do), but the truth concerning obedience is not even understood, because the intimacy of every word from the Holy Spirit comes in higher than our current understanding of *obey*. As we read the Word of God, the Holy Spirit will begin to reveal deep truths to our spirits concerning how we relate to Him.

During this fellowship, He reveals more of the intimate relationship that He desires to have with us through other Scriptures, so that our understanding and wisdom are completed with the language of love—a willing heart that is totally yielded to the voice of the Holy Spirit.

The Holy Spirit brought up to me (even while writing these words) the story of David's men getting him some water. The retrieval of water from behind enemy lines was motivated solely from a longing that David voiced because he was thirsty. He did not command in the sense of how most people understand the word *command*. He simply, voiced a desire. The men acted on it, not counting the risk or the level of security and brought water back to him. It was as though their very life and blood had paid for the cost of the water for David, who could not even drink it, for it was too precious. These men were yielded. In like manner we might say today that we listened to the voice of the Holy Spirit. They had the pulse of the Father's heart and acted without regard to their own lives in the circumstance, in order to please and serve their King. It was an act of love. Jesus said that if you obey Me you will love Me, and if you love Me you will obey Me. Obedience is the foundation, but it is just the beginning of learning the love language. Those who are walking in love do yield and surrender to Him. They listen intimately to the Holy Spirit and place the finishing touches on what He is doing—since love is the highest purpose for all that He is doing.

As we take a closer look at the four dimensions: *width, length, depth,* and *height,* we can see the importance of why the Father reveals these secrets of the kingdom. The *width* that we experience in His glory could be said in this way, "Whatever worked in your hometown in America, works anywhere, no matter where your country may be or wherever you place the soles of your feet." *Length* is described as a dimension of time. Whatever worked before, works now and forever. "Jesus Christ is the same yesterday, today, and forever" (Hebrews 13:8 NKJV).

The Holy Spirit searches all of the *deep* things of God. He wants our experiences in Christ to be so rich, and full of the nature of the Father, that we are manifesting His glory in all we say and do. "Therefore, whether you eat or drink, or whatever you do, do all to the glory of God" (1 Corinthians 10:31 NKJV). All the ways and thoughts of the Father are higher than ours. This dimension in *height* is superlative in every way. These words were expressed in Jesus' prayer in John 17.

Jesus said with clarity how much He desires for our ways: our words and our works, to be one with Him and the Father. He restored the glory so that we would be given His glory as a gift from the Father. This gift, which is presented in salvation, we have inherited from the Father who has qualified us to enter this realm—the kingdom of light—the kingdom of His glory. The assertive language in His prayer is that He desired to give us the same glory He had with the Father before establishing the very foundations of this world. That glory is what established the worlds!

God, who at various times and in various ways spoke in time past to the fathers by the prophets, has in these last days spoken to us by His Son, whom He has appointed heir of all things, through whom also He made the worlds; who being the brightness of His glory and the express image of His person, and upholding all things by the word of His power, when He had by Himself purged our sins, sat down at the right hand of the Majesty on high, (Hebrews 1:1–3 NKJV)

The wisdom from the heart of the Father being revealed through the words of Jesus expresses what has always been the Father's plan: that *in Christ* we would experience the same glory. That is the reality and the truth found in the gospel that is not known throughout the whole church, let alone the whole world. Jesus further said that He wants to perfect in us all of our experiences and wisdom concerning His glory.

That they all may be one, as You, Father, are in Me, and I in You; that they also may be one in Us, that the world may believe that You sent Me. And the glory which You gave Me I have given them, that they may be one just as We are one: I in them, and You in Me; that they may be made perfect in one, and that the world may know that You have sent Me, and have loved them as You have loved Me. Father, I desire that they also whom You gave Me may be with Me where I am, that they may behold My glory which You have given Me; for You loved Me before the foundation of the world. (John 17:21–24 NKJV)

Finally, with the deepest heartfelt desires that could be expressed, Jesus declared that He desires the same intimate experience that He has always known, to be ours as well. He wants to bring us up higher, to the very Throne of Glory, so that all that is available to Jesus would be given to us and made our experience too. "He raises the poor from the dust and lifts the beggar from the ash heap, to set them among princes and make them inherit the throne of glory" (1 Samuel 2:8 NKJV).

This stretches the imagination beyond belief for the natural man. The old nature cannot believe the possibility, the reality, even the truth in Jesus' words. The new creation, the nature of Christ in us and our relationship in Christ, completes and breathes life into our spiritual nature first, and transforms our thinking second. You and I need the wisdom from the Holy Spirit to be able to comprehend all that is on the Father's heart and mind.

Jesus is seated in heavenly places. He is seated on the very Throne of Glory. Paul, also said that we too are seated with Him in heavenly places. The timeframe for being with Him in heavenly places is *now*, though in our minds it does not seem practical. It seems less a reality in our lives because our minds are more subject to follow the senses rather than the Word of God. His Truth to the natural world we live in is indeed true both in this physical world and the spiritual world.

But God, who is rich in mercy, because of His great love with which He loved us, even when we were dead in trespasses, made us alive together with Christ (by grace you have been saved), and raised us up together, and made us sit together in the heavenly places in Christ Jesus, that in the ages to come He might show the exceeding riches of His grace in His kindness toward us in Christ Jesus. (Ephesians 2:4–7 NKJV)

3

I've Fallen and Can't Get Up

H ow does something invisible become the living reality in this visible realm? The Father's wisdom that is being revealed through Jesus, and continues to be revealed by the Holy Spirit in us, is consistent through His word. We understand that the things which are visible have been made through the things that are invisible. This relation with His word came from the invisible realm. His word is always in the invisible realm of His glory. We are given access and wisdom to understand how to manifest His glory by how the Holy Spirit reveals this intimate knowledge to our spirits.

Jesus created a relationship so refined, so pure, and so holy for us that we come to Him as we are, and leave as He is. The reality of the relationship that we have with the Father is seen clearly through every word, every *pearl* that the Holy Spirit makes known to us. We receive revelation in the spiritual realm and experience its reality in the physical realm. Jesus prayed these life-giving words in the garden.

And the glory which You gave Me I have given them, that they may be one just as We are one: I in them, and You in Me; that they may be made perfect in one, and that the world may know that You have sent Me, and have loved them as You have loved Me. (John 17:22, 23 NKJV)

These two verses alone are so rich that we could not possibly unveil all the riches found in them. Although this is true of every word from the Father, we capture the reality that we receive the same glory Jesus received when He makes it known to us. Jesus also clearly said that we are being perfected in what He gave us, what had been deposited within us. Our ability to receive the revelation that we are loved by the Father in the same way He loves Jesus, transforms the results, especially in the area of prayer. Jesus prayed, "I thank you Father, that You always hear Me." This becomes our experience as well, no matter how great the difficulty that is set before us.

An experience I had years ago, shortly after I had become a believer, expresses this transforming nature of Christ in us. A good friend of mine who had been in the US Army was coming home on leave. I knew that I would be spending time with him, although I had become a Christian after I had last seen him. It is also noteworthy, how the enemy will try to use Scripture against us, not unlike how he had done with Jesus. I read a verse in Proverbs that stated, "Never forsake your friends, nor your father's friends." I truly believe that the Father will prune away those who will hinder our walk, and because of their own desires, they will go their own separate ways. When I first read that verse, I knew that

I did not want to forsake any friends, but I also knew I was willing to do things that I would not now even consider, let alone do. The Holy Spirit perfects us even as our heavenly Father is perfect.

We get nudges and reminders all the time from the Holy Spirit, yet at the time we may not have our ears tuned to know it was Him. A long time before my friend ever came home on leave, I was already getting insight from the Holy Spirit. He kept showing me that my old way of life was coming to an end, and that I would no longer be participating in those things. We will get constant challenges to our thinking until we have the Word answer that is engrafted and fused to our souls. In Ephesians 6:13, we read, "…having done everything, to stand. Stand therefore…" We have to make His word in us as real as it is in Him. We have to say *no,* and let our *no* mean no, and our *yes* mean yes.

After my friend Steve arrived in the area we did many things to reconnect with the *good ole times,* but I kept running into dead end paths. I was still underage and out in the hills having a beer with him one evening. One would think that because we were way out in the countryside we would be alright. While in the vehicle, sipping on a beer and, lo and behold, a state police officer came driving way out there and spotted us sitting a short distance from the road. He backed up and then pulled up to where we were parked. This was my first warning from the Lord. The officer gave me a ticket for having empty beer bottles in the vehicle, as a minor in consumption. I had the embarrassment of going to court over the matter too.

One would also think that particular fiasco would jumpstart my thinking, but some of us have much more pride and stubbornness in us than we are willing to admit. Again, I was with this same friend while he was still on leave, only this time we were hanging out all day together at various friends' homes, drinking and partying, including different drugs that were available. In the evening we went out joyriding, listening to music, and enjoying time with a couple of girlfriends. While parked off the road, out in the country-side again, I got out of the car because nature called. Upon returning, I leaned with my hand against the side of the vehicle for support. Suddenly, my hand slipped away from the car, and I fell face down into the mud and gravel. I didn't move at all, nor had I braced my fall.

While I was lying on the ground, I heard this voice distinctively, *'God sees what you are doing; He will forgive you.'* Although, when I first heard it, it did not ring with truth. It had the same kind of tone as when I read those words in Proverbs about never forsaking your friends—very subtle. It would have hardly been noticeable had the Holy Spirit not intervened. Still lying there late at night, in that mud and gravel alongside the vehicle, I also heard this voice, *'What are you going to do, continue doing these things, or follow Me?'* This time I knew immediately—that was the voice of the Lord. It was the Spirit's voice to awaken me. I sensed this was almost a life and death matter that demanded a choice by me. I made that choice within my heart, but I said nothing. The decision was this: *No, I am not doing these things anymore!* Suddenly, I was completely sober. It was an immediate and dramatic change. All I had done was make a choice in my heart, yielding to what He had asked me, and supernaturally, instantly, I was changed.

I got back up and sat inside the car, hardly saying another word the rest of the night. Those in the car with me all kind of laughed, because they saw the mud on the side of my face. I had a New Testament in my back pocket that I pulled out a couple times to read, but never said a word to anyone. About three days later, I discovered the following passages from Lamentations and was totally amazed at how this had been my exact experience, as if those verses had been freshly written just for me.

The Lord is good to those who wait for Him, to the soul who seeks Him. It is good that one should hope and wait quietly for the salvation of the Lord. It is good for a man to bear the yoke in his youth. Let him sit alone and keep silent, because God has laid it on him; let him put his mouth in the dust—there may yet be hope. Let him give his cheek to the one who strikes him, and be full of reproach. For the Lord will not cast off forever. Though He causes grief, yet He will show compassion according to the multitude of His mercies. (Lamentations 3:25-32 NKJV)

We have the "*nothing is impossible*" glory in us, on our behalf, perfecting us in our understanding of how He loves us the same as He loves Jesus. Another noteworthy observation is *that the world will know that the Father has sent Jesus* (John 17:23). This understanding is being perfected within us too. We know already by subjective experience (though Jesus is opening wide the experiences we have in His glory) that it would be objective to reach out beyond the lives of all those who are around us. They see and experience the same glory which is in Jesus, now being manifested through us with the same efficacious nature that we have come to understand. This truly testifies as to how His glory manifested then, and how it continues to manifest now through us, proving that the Father has sent Jesus, the Lord of Glory, into the world.

Our relationship with the Father can be portrayed as His children sitting on the Father's lap. He asks us about what we see with our eyes and hear with our ears. He gives us an opportunity to decide and answer based upon those observations, whether or not it lines up with what He has already revealed to us. He has authorized us to make voiced COMMANDS from His Throne that creatively change whatever is NOT good, NOT acceptable, and NOT perfect, by releasing His glory in our words.

Even if what we saw was totally dark and evil, it would make no difference, because anytime the Father asks us a question, His wisdom and His glory are immediately available to us by the Holy Spirit. Our heart is in tune; therefore, it is Spirit to spirit language that we are receiving. We are being graced with the wisdom, revelation, and the knowledge of the glory in that very moment, which means we DECIDE based upon heart choices that are centered on how well we know the Father's heart.

4

Into the Firmament

$\mathcal{N}$ otice the clear language from Jesus' prayer in John 17, "Father, I desire that they also whom You gave Me may be with Me where I am, that they may behold My glory which You have given Me; for You loved Me before the foundation of the world" (John 17:24 NKJV). The language, that Jesus gave to us the same glory that He received, had already been revealed in verse 22. Now we are seeing experientially how it is being manifested. This had always been Jesus' desire. It is our inheritance as children of light and sons of glory to be privileged to enjoy what Jesus had always enjoyed with the Father.

This stream of His glory—this stream of life through us—can be illustrated in many ways, but He has chosen some simple ways so that it would not be missed. The river that flows from the throne as described in Ezekiel, chapter 47, outlines the truth of how everything flows from the Father of glory. As this river is traced and walked out in the Scripture, at each interval where it is crossed it becomes deeper. This is not unlike our own walk in the Spirit; at first, we experience simple things in the spirit realm as we wade out only ankle deep; as we continue on, the water rises up to our knees; further out, we gain some confidence and experiencing at a waist-high level; and finally, we cross through His stream of glory and we can no longer touch the bottom. His glory surrounds us, and we are flowing in His stream wherever the current takes us. This possibility exists now. It is experienced often in corporate worship, as well as individually, according to how we avail ourselves to the Holy Spirit and with prayer. This communing with Him, and He with us, transforms our lives. Not only does it transform our lives, but it also transforms the lives of those around us. His glory should flow into all that we say and do, wherever we place the soles of our feet.

The exact nature and purpose of this book, *Riches of Glory,* is for you to be established and move seamlessly into all the realms of God's glory. Beginning at the subatomic level, His Word begins to radiate within your spirit. This is the imperishable Seed which has birthed you into the kingdom of light—the kingdom of glory.

For you have been born again, not of perishable seed, but of imperishable, through the living and enduring word of God. (1 Peter 1:23 NIV)

But as many as received him, to them gave he power to become the sons of God, even to them that believe on his name: (John 1:12 KJV)

And my speech and my preaching were not with persuasive words of human wisdom, but in demonstration of the Spirit and of power, that your faith should not be in the wisdom of men but in the power of God. (I Corinthians 2:4, 5 NKJV)

We are born of imperishable seed, but as long as the seed remains inactive and not germinated, then nothing manifests. What Jesus did was command His glory into us. If this seed only remains inactive, in a state of hope, then it coincides with what the Scripture states, "Christ in you, the hope of glory." As long as this is only a hope, though it is true that He is in you, because His glory is inactive, it remains in a dormant state. Jesus said "...out of the good treasure of his heart produces good things" (Matthew 12:35). That treasure—His glory—is what was deposited in us. He gave wisdom as to how this treasure would be useful, producing more good things that would come from within our lives. It is through the abundance of our heart that our mouth speaks. This treasure is confirmed by, "But we have this treasure in earthen vessels, that the excellence of the power may be of God and not of us" (2 Corinthians 4:7 NKJV).

This treasure is in our earthen vessel now, not when we get a glorified vessel. We are fellow-workers with the Father of glory, manifesting His glory wherever we go. He restored the glory. Now, we restore His glory wherever we go, in all that we say and do. When a leg straightens out that was all twisted—that is His glory. When a tree grows from a dead stick—that is His glory. When someone is desperate and loses all hope, but is stopped in their tracks from making a terrible decision—that is His glory. When every miracle takes place to confirm the word that we declare—that is His glory.

We can have as much of His glory as we desire, "...as much as they wanted." There are a couple verses that are easy to remember and shed light on this more, "And Jesus took the loaves, and when He had given thanks He distributed them to the disciples, and the disciples to those sitting down; and likewise of the fish, as much as they wanted" (John 6:11 NKJV). "At the festivals and the appointed feast days the grain offering shall be an ephah for a bull, an ephah for a ram, as much as he wants to give for the lambs, and a hin of oil with every ephah" (Ezekiel 46:11 NKJV). We can have as much of the Lamb of God as we desire. He wants us to deliberately, assertively, and aggressively take from Him.

Every Word He declares is so rich that you may feed continually from that one word and never exhaust all of this wisdom of His glory that was richly poured into it. It is the way to discern whether it is His word or not, because of His Spirit and His glory which are manifested give us insight. The way to tell how what He said is a reality and the truth or not, is by simply placing His word in your mouth and it manifests. It must become one with your spirit to manifest. Now it is His life directly flowing through all of your words.

An evangelistic team came through here some time ago. They would pray in the spirit every morning for almost an hour, which supercharged their spirit-man. Afterwards, they were experiencing greater glory in all their activities. I agree, and understand this, since I pray in the spirit throughout the day. When we choose deliberately to pray in the spirit each morning, then we too will be so overflowing with His power and presence that His glory will be radiating out of us. Like Jesus, we can expect power to come out of us and heal them all. "And the whole multitude sought to touch Him, for power went out from Him and healed them all" (Luke 6:19 NKJV).

The relationship in this Spirit to spirit language must be permeated with Him. Uniquely, He has taken appropriate action by giving us His glory to bond and permeate our spirits as one. The wisdom and knowledge that the Holy Spirit teaches concerning His glory is extremely valuable, not only in this life, but in the life to come. These are the treasures that we have inherited. These treasures are imparted and given to us freely. What He has freely given to us, we can freely give to others. The ministry of reconciliation is all about restoring His glory in every realm of life.

We work together with the Holy Spirit. He helps us, and we are yielded to Him. Together we become that spiritual life-force of the Father's glory that has the kingdom of darkness in disarray. Every activity by the enemy (like those birds in the parable of the sower) is aimed at dislodging any revelation from the Holy Spirit and lessening its effect if possible. We are sensitive because of the Holy Spirit's work in us to see those areas around us that need the word of reconciliation to be restored to its rightful place in His garden. We should understand that this *terra firma* beneath us responds to seeds that we plant. Jesus declared "The sower sows the seed," which then from His own commentary on His own parable said, "The sower sows the word." In truth, He said that we not only plant in the *terra firma*, we also plant in this atmosphere above called *firmament* in Genesis by the words we speak. So that what we speak grows. We have super seeds within His glory. Unlike other kinds of seeds, these produce an immediate harvest.

Every word that comes from the Holy Spirit in reality came from the Father of glory. It is totally amazing to capture the way Jesus thought through the words He spoke. "All things that the Father has (imagine everything the Father has) are Mine. Therefore I said that He (the Holy Spirit) will take of Mine and declare *it* to you" (John 16:15 NKJV). Now imagine what the Holy Spirit declares and speaks to us. This is the creative language that the Father speaks. He formed the whole universe with His spoken words. Then Jesus tells us that His words are to be in our mouth. Now we know exactly what kind of words we speak. They have the creative authority from the Father of glory. The words spoken to us by the Holy Spirit have this authority; therefore, being carefully attentive and being totally yielded to the voice of the Holy Spirit is everything! "He who has ears to hear let him hear."

We don't want to be the kind of people who sing the dirge, though this seems to be what is heard most everywhere we go. He has called us into a much higher relationship, operating with His wisdom from the throne. Jesus was raised from the dead by the glory of the Father. That joy of the resurrection power should resonate through our lives personally, presently, and ever-increasingly, not just

repeated only with words of historical accuracy. The whole
purpose and joy of coming together is fulfilling the royal law
of love that builds up one another for this ministry of
reconciliation—the ministry to restore all things.

> For the creation waits with eager longing for the revealing
> of the sons of God. For the creation was subjected to
> futility, not willingly, but because of him who subjected it,
> in hope that the creation itself will be set free from its
> bondage to corruption and obtain the freedom of the glory
> of the children of God. (Romans 8:19–21 ESV)

We are not following the voice of men, but are acutely
training the inner man to know and follow the voice of the
Holy Spirit in all things. The stabilized condition of the
believer is when Christ has come into our lives, and we have
stepped into His life. That reminder from Jesus, "I abide in
you, and you abide in Me", by taking communion as often as
we do, is firmly establishing these truths within us—we are
one with Him. It is not the act that reminds as much as it is
the truth in Him that reminds us we are one. The act of
communion dramatizes what is already true in the spirit, and
renews the mind. It also engages our own spirit deliberately
to act in faith, stand by grace, and rejoice in the hope of His
glory being manifested.

Put greater emphasis on Him, for Him, in Him, and to
Him in our lives, more than anything else that we would do.
Such as, the communion He has chosen that we enjoy as
one with Him. You remain in Him. That word *remain* is
another word for *abide*, or how I have said, "Permeated with

Him and with His word." Our focus is on Him, now and forever, not on what the enemy is doing or not doing. Sin-consciousness or being conscious of sin all the time, only produces more sin. Righteousness-consciousness produces in us an overflow of His glory that transforms everything around us, and restores His glory wherever we go. This is the work and ministry that is produced by the Holy Spirit, reminding us that we are righteous in Him.

5

Under the Light

I n Peter, we can understand how powerful His word is. "Like newborn babies, crave pure spiritual milk, so that by it you may grow up in your salvation, now that you have tasted that the Lord is good" (1 Peter 2:2, 3 NIV). The word *crave* is a deep seated desire, because of how much time has been spent to develop that desire. This is what He expects to become a living reality within us. Another form of that word crave would be lust, which means a passionate, overpowering desire to crave. Most people's minds gravitate to some sexual desire because of how the word has often been used. In truth, it is the deep passionate desire for Him and for His word that should be so developed within us that it drives us to willingly please Him in all we say and do. The saturation point of His word is never reached, but continues to be this strong craving for more of Him. It is developed by following the voice of the Holy Spirit. *Earnestly desire* and *greatly long for* are those phrases that should be the living truth at the root of His love in us becoming activated, so that we live, breathe, eat, and sleep constantly craving more of Him.

Human emotions that are connected in a relationship are very similar, but when birthed in the spirit realm within us, these emotions are much higher and deeper, with the ability to endure long-suffering beyond all measure, until His glory is manifested. The grace in His glory is what propagates the necessary development within us. He that is forgiven of much, loves much! The reality of knowing how much He has forgiven us ignites His love with which He has flooded our spirit, so that it begins to overflow into all our thoughts, emotions, and volitions. I think that the depth of His love truly perfects what we imagine we might be able to do. His love bends our wills, stretches our imaginations, and develops our ability to see things how He sees things. It reveals His heart and perfects our ability to clearly hear His voice and follow His leading. Mostly, what blinds us from knowing this depth of His forgiveness and love is our own pride. We have pride within us that still entangles our thinking with the belief that we could have, should have, and would have done better. Those beliefs come from the old nature.

When Jesus made these statements about Himself, *I only do what I see the Father doing. I only say what I hear the Father saying*, they capture the language of love that is being perfected in us. He walked in love with the Father. The Father is totally into Him, and He is totally into the Father. This is very true! Yet the mind of man filtered with religion comes no where near the true relationship with Him. Immaturity has been expressed by the church overall because our words have been coming in too low. Although these filtered words have established faith, they lacked the purity and power to bring others up higher into this wonderful knowledge of His glory. When we wield this sword of the spirit, the depths and riches of His glory being expressed, brings everyone up higher into the presence of the Father. Jesus said very clearly, "And I, if I be lifted up from the earth, will draw all *men* unto me" (John 12:32 KJV). But if we accurately measure this by asking ourselves if all men are being drawn to Him, it is revealed that we have not truly understood this knowledge of the glory, which is far above all the heavens and the earth, for His glory is above all the heavens and the earth.

This had been a hunger within me, a craving for more of His word that He had ignited already, even before I had been born-again. I think one of the earmarks of any believer is that they would have such a hunger for His word. Not long after I had been saved, this new awakened desire became a delight for reading His word. I truly hungered, wanting to hear and know what the Spirit was saying. "Blessed are those who hunger and thirst for righteousness, for they shall be filled" (Matthew 5:6 NKJV).

When I was living at home, my dad had house rules that the lights were out after a certain time at night, (usually 11:00pm). On one occasion I still wanted to read, so I got dressed and went out for a walk. It was one of those gloomy nights, filled with rain clouds, and the moon was just a sliver in the sky. Black clouds blotted out all the light that might have been available. I had walked a few miles looking for a place with enough light where I could sit and read my Bible when I came to a restaurant that was closed (it was after hours). There was a streetlight next to the restaurant that made reading possible, so I sat on the steps at three in the morning just reading. A few moments later a state police officer pulled up in the parking lot. He asked me what I was doing.

Naively, I did not even consider how the scene may have appeared to him, but told him the truth. "I wanted to read my Bible, and it seemed like a good place for me because of the streetlights that made it possible for me to see what I was reading."

He said, "It's probably not a good idea to sit on the steps of this business, since it is closed. Others might have different thoughts about why you are here."

I think that in pursuing Him, (as the song goes) the things of the earth grow strangely dim. We have more of His word in us than the ways of the world. At times it may appear that we are strange, but He is directing our lives. It is for His glory that we walk after the dictates of our heart. The Word declares in the book of Proverbs, "The spirit of a man is the lamp of the Lord, searching all the inner depths of his heart" (Proverbs 20:27 NKJV). Our spirit becomes a safe guide in the hands of the Lord, because He has placed a new spirit within us. He has also given us the Holy Spirit to teach us all of His ways and perfect the knowledge of His glory in us.

Unto you therefore which believe He is precious: but unto them which be disobedient, the stone which the builders disallowed, the same is made the head of the corner, and a stone of stumbling, and a rock of offense, even to them which stumble at the word, being disobedient: whereunto also they were appointed. But ye are a chosen generation a royal priesthood, an holy nation, a peculiar people; that ye should shew forth the praises of Him who hath called you out of darkness into His marvelous light. (1 Peter 2:7–9 KJV)

Communion, at every level in the disciple's growth, takes care of every area in the life of the believer. The humility in receiving communion engages that simple act of faith to believe and the grace that is received. It is fruitful as the simplest form of prayer, meditation, and worship. The wisdom from the Holy Spirit, because He has captured and arrested our attention, begins to transform each and every thought that is weighed out in the light of His glory.

Meditate on the power of One. We are one with Him because of the glory He gave us. We act in the power of One. It is the nature of this new creation. We, individually, can act on the power of One because we know that apart from Him we can do nothing. To state this as a specific word from the Holy Spirit to me personally, I would say, "I am One with the Father. All that You have, has been given to Jesus, and the Holy Spirit is revealing to me now that same wisdom that You, Father possess. I thank you, Father for Your wisdom, I thank you, Father for Your favor."

Meditate on Him allowing the truth of His nature to permeate yours. His nature is already alive in you. You are just actively partaking of His divine nature through those promises that the Holy Spirit ignites within you. It adjusts what is of Him and what is of the old nature. "By which have been given to us exceedingly great and precious promises, that through these you may be partakers of the divine nature, having escaped the corruption that is in the world through lust" (2 Peter 1:4 NKJV).

Romans 8:18 is the verse that the Holy Spirit unveiled to me over a period of four years as He began to teach me on the glory. He gave me very private tutoring lessons specifically designed and created for me, to reveal this knowledge of His glory. I meditated on that verse everyday for those four years. I did not make a decision to meditate that long on a single verse; that is just how He was leading me. Everything that you are reading in this book and the entire book series, came out of the time spent meditating on that one verse, and as He bonded other verses together with it. *"For I consider that the sufferings of this present time are not worthy to be compared with the glory which shall be revealed in us"* (Romans 8:18 NKJV).

We simply receive all that is true in Him, the condition that already exists in our spirit, so that our minds can accurately dial into that same Holy Spirit *frequency.* Taking communion helps solidify this within our minds because of how deceitful that old nature is. We are not the sick trying to get well; we are healed already. "Let the weak say, 'I am strong'" (Joel 3:10 NKJV). It is not a fantasy in the mind to pretend we are healed. "...by His stripes we were healed" (Isaiah 53:5 NKJV). It is the condition of releasing His glory, which He has deposited in us. The Holy Spirit is deeply expressing that truth to us. We can accomplish glorious things together by the alignment of our words with His wisdom.

Riches of Glory

6

Blood-Stained Hands

O nce when I was taking communion, I was settling within me the solemn commitment I have towards the Father. As I was sitting there with the drink and the bread in my hand, the Holy Spirit asked me a question concerning what I was holding. I answered in this way, "The bread represents Your body that was broken for me." I ate, and the Holy Spirit interjected this thought, "Those are the teeth that gnashed at Me and spoke out against Me." It was humbling to say the least, because we have all gone astray and we were against Him.

While still sitting there in silence, listening more attentively, the Holy Spirit spoke to me again concerning communion, "What are you holding in your hand?" I had the communion cup in my hand, and while not particularly noticing it, my thumb was on the rim of the cup and some of the juice touched my thumb. I answered the Holy Spirit, "The blood which was shed for me." Again the Holy Spirit interjected a thought to me, "Those are the hands that are stained with spilling My blood." These words from the Holy Spirit did not have an attitude of condemnation. He was allowing me to know that I was no different than those who had actually nailed Jesus to the cross. That spirit within them was the same old nature resident within me; however, in much love and carefulness He had qualified not only me, but also all those who call upon His Name to enjoy the fruits of Jesus' labor.

Imagine that you had a carpet which had been stained, and nothing that you ever tried would clean up the stain. When Christ came He cleaned up every one of the stains in our lives. His life blood is the only thing in the entire universe that ever will. He had transformed the blood He offered as sacrifice and presented it before the Father, so that the Father gave Him glory. Jesus' glory is the very thing He gave us that has now not only cleaned up our stained lives but continues to clean up all of our stains.

We are carrying within us this very *active ingredient*—the dying of Christ—the agent that cleans up these kinds of stains. And while His glory within us is being converted through our words, we too are expressing and expanding this stain removal ability which thoroughly cleanses like nothing else through this knowledge of His glory that we speak. "If you forgive the sins of any, they are forgiven them; if you retain the sins of any, they are retained" (John 20:23 NKJV).

He wanted me to know that without Him, I can do nothing. "I am the vine, you are the branches. He who abides in Me, and I in him, bears much fruit; for without Me you can do nothing. If anyone does not abide in Me, he is cast out as a branch and is withered; and they gather them and throw them into the fire, and they are burned" (John 15:5, 6 NKJV). He is the Lord of Glory, and because they did not know who He was, they crucified Him. Every time we do not know who He is in our lives, we crucify Him all over again. He healed us by His stripes. When we do not know this to be the truth, we crucify Him all over again.

The pattern of conversion from the Father can be followed simply enough through understanding His glory. The Father sent the Son, and the Son died destroying sin in His body forever. The Father received this sacrifice with His pure blood and gave Him glory. Jesus gave this glory to us when we called on His name. The Holy Spirit activates His glory in us with the knowledge of the glory. That glory is activated and converted into our words. His glory is released into every realm He assigned us to; it is the fruit (results) produced from His words that have been converted in our mouths. These glory-filled words go back to the Father and do not return to Him void of an answer, but accomplish (through us) what He sends them out to do (Isaiah 55:11).

There is no time or distance in His glory, and His glory knows no boundaries, so His glory in your mouth will know no boundaries either. The components regarding time and how far His glory has removed all stains can be understood when we come into alignment with Him in our thinking. Our eyes see differently than how He sees. Our ears hear differently than how He hears. That is why the Holy Spirit must train us to see the reality that is already in the spirit realm—His glory.

That first reality we are to see is that we are already with Him on the Throne of Glory. "A glorious high throne from the beginning is the place of our sanctuary" (Jeremiah 17:12 NKJV). It has been from the beginning of time. Because He removed the stains, we can now see clearly from the beginning of time with Him. We have total peace and joy from that place, His Throne of Glory. When we have peace and joy now, it is an expression that our minds are being renewed. We have come to understand that our spirits are already sitting on the Throne of Glory in Christ. We are ruling and reigning in this spiritual realm—His glory.

Whatever the Lord has done, His glory does, for He is one with His glory. His glory does the same through us, but we do not know this yet since we have not tasted those promises (and seen them manifest) in our own intimate experiences in Christ. It is the purpose of the Holy Spirit to teach and train so that it becomes a consistent reality within our own experiences. "This is the day the Lord has made; we will rejoice and be glad in it" (Psalm 118:24 NKJV). Now we can say the Lord rejoiced before time began, so that we would reign with Him while experiencing all that He and the Father have always known. The Lord designs and makes each day. His glory is one with Him; therefore, His glory designs each day. When we pray and declare, we are designing days together with Him.

In the realm He has assigned to you and I, even the days will respond to His glory according to what we plant together with Him by sowing with our mouth in prayer and declaring. Without Him we can do nothing. With Him nothing is impossible. The Holy Spirit teaches us how to yield to Him so that these promises become a reality within us to produce *pearls*. He has declared that we are now clean from all stains. That declaration is timeless, and He has taken the keys of hell and death from the enemy. Those keys are stains that have to be removed from our thinking for us to benefit from all the work of the Father. Remember, He is the author and the finisher of our story. When did our story first begin, on our birthday? No, our story began before time began. The Lamb of God was slain for our stains before the world began.

Now all the way back in time, no stains, and all the way forward in time, no stains. No matter how far back in time you imagine, there are no boundaries in His glory. It is timeless in His glory. "Then your light shall break forth like the morning, your healing shall spring forth speedily, and your righteousness shall go before you; the glory of the Lord shall be your rear guard" (Isaiah 58:8 NKJV). His righteousness is going how far into the future before us? As far as His glory is our rear guard, so shall His righteousness go before us. In the same way He is one with His glory, this is true of His righteousness. We have become the righteousness of God in Christ.

Jesus' greatest desire was eternally realized when He had gone to the cross. When He was raised from the grave and given glory, His joy came from what He received. Now He has imparted to us forever; the Holy Spirit is with us forever. We are being tempered by Him to be completely renewed in every thought, to enter His glory in every promise, and to enjoy His divine nature—His glory. "Jesus Christ is the same yesterday, today, and forever" (Hebrews 13:8 NKJV). Jesus has cleaned all the stains, so that we are free from anything the enemy has.

We are learning to clean the stains with Him, and by the power of His glory, we now see them as only deceptions from the enemy. "He who sins is of the devil, for the devil has sinned from the beginning. For this purpose the Son of God was manifested, that He might destroy the works of the devil" (1 John 3:8 NKJV). We, however, are taking the cleansing agent—His blood and glory—to clean up every realm He has assigned to us. "That He might sanctify and cleanse her with the washing of water by the word" (Ephesians 5:26 NKJV).

The conversion within us should be in everything, not just in the reality that we are born-again. It should show up in the way we see, hear, and speak about things, e.g., hundreds of years ago people believed that the world was flat. Had we lived back then, everyone we met would have told us the world was flat. If someone were to go out to sea and went too far, it was believed they would fall off the edge of the world. Until the truth was revealed that the world was not flat, but in spherical form, then the old way of thinking had not changed. Minds were not converted to the truth. Now, with this knowledge of the glory, it is no different. If we only see things and hear things from a fragmented truth, we do not have the fullness of the glory knowledge which comes in higher than anything else. When Jesus performed the miracle of multiplying the bread and the fish, He told the disciples to *gather up the fragments that none be lost (John 6:12).* Glory was manifested, and He tells us today the very same, gather up the fragments of His word, so that none is lost concerning His glory.

We must see that He was raised from the dead to be empowered in salvation! The words that Jesus spoke before the cross were ratified by the Father. We are raised from the dead in the same way that He had been raised by the glory of the Father. It is this glory that gives us a new way of life. The glory connects in us heaven and earth. We must see Christ seated in the heavenly places to be perfected in Him! We are seated with Him.

But we speak the wisdom of God in a mystery, the hidden wisdom which God ordained before the ages for our glory, which none of the rulers of this age knew; for had they known, they would not have crucified the Lord of glory. (1 Corinthians 2:7, 8 NKJV)

Therefore we were buried with Him through baptism into death, that just as Christ was raised from the dead by the glory of the Father, even so we also should walk in newness of life. (Romans 6:4 NKJV)

But God, who is rich in mercy, because of His great love with which He loved us, even when we were dead in trespasses, made us alive together with Christ (by grace you have been saved), and raised us up together, and made us sit together in the heavenly places in Christ Jesus. (Ephesians 2:4-6 NKJV)

7

You Are Releasing Life

*O*ne time I was discussing with young believers about the quality of choices that they could make regarding to participate or not participate with their peers. I made it clear as to how those choices should come from relationships that are built on love, and that those choices would be revealed by the things they spoke and believed. For instance, let's say a drinking party and hanging with friends was being promoted, and the rule from home was not to be with others who are drinking under age. The best choice would be demonstrated in response to the invitation, "I love my parents so much that I do not want to bring them any displeasure, so I cannot go to this party with all of you." The decision was made and voiced from a position of love—their relationship with their parents—not from what rules they should obey or not obey. The love language always comes in higher.

After I had lived in Florida for a while, two of my friends and I prayed and fasted. The Holy Spirit set apart a friend, Ron, to accompany me to Massachusetts. Ron was from that area before becoming a Christian. I stayed up there for almost four months but before he left to come back, (he was there for two weeks) we went to his original church where he grew up. He was raised as a Catholic so we went to the Catholic Church. Now I was never raised a Catholic so during mass, I reasoned: *I am here with him, so I will just do what he does.*

When it was time for communion (Holy Eucharist as they called it), all of us who were going to partake in communion were standing in a column facing the front. I'm a believer so I decided to take communion. While waiting in line, I couldn't see what those in front of me were doing. One person went, then another, until I was finally standing at the front ready to take communion. I've never taken communion in a Catholic Church. While I was standing up there, the two altar boys were also standing facing me. One held out a bowl of the tiny wafers. I reached in to take one of those wafers, but my hand was slapped by the priest. I thought for a brief moment: *he must think I'm going to take more than my share.* That's how I had reasoned. Then I thought: *well I know me, I'm not going to take more than my share.* So I reached again, and my hand was immediately slapped down. I had imagined: *well wait a sec, he can't be that naïve.* I reached once more for a wafer, only this time when the priest slapped my hand, it was hard enough that all of those wafers went floating up into the air like little feathers everywhere. The altar boys with their little brass spoons were trying to scoop them all up before they fell to the carpet.

The priest gave me that certain curious look like a praying mantis looking sideways and said, "I want to talk to you after the mass." After mass, my friend, Ron, and I, were standing there talking with the priest. Ron explained, "This guy, this brother was saved like Paul of Tarsus." He diffused the situation that was created by my own lack of understanding in partaking communion in the Catholic mass. The priest explained to me the misunderstanding. What he said to me was kind of interesting, "When you reached in (to grab a wafer) that would be *take,* but the way that we were taught is to receive." Their receiving would be this way: you stick your tongue out and the priest places the wafer on it. Receive! There are two things that need to be understood in our lives from some of that imagery.

One of the promises reveals these images from Matthew 13:33, "The kingdom of heaven is like yeast that a woman *took...*" That *take* or *took* in that verse is an aggressive, assertive take. So if I was doing that during communion at Ron's church I would have reached and grabbed all of them! That's the kind of assertiveness He wants us to have as we reach in for every promise—assertive, aggressive *take.* I own it! That's *my* promise. This is *my* Lord. That's *my* inheritance. It has to be that alive inside our hearts with that kind of tenacity, and it has to be unwavering; however, in the walk of those who are yielding to the Holy Spirit, assertiveness is done only in humility. We are not drawing attention to ourselves. We are always drawing attention to Jesus and giving glory to the Father, learning how to **receive** from Him and how to **release** with Him.

The basis for understanding the new creation is not from what you can't have or can't do, but in reality only following His voice. The uncomplicated and simple new life becomes so much more an act of love in every stride. You will notice its impact in all areas of your life, having victory in areas that seemed the weakest. This is very true! This is why I always say about our walk that it's *obedience to faith, following the voice of the Holy Spirit.* This love walk has deeper connectivity in the spirit, and has pure heart motives which are far above written instructions.

The desire to listen to the Holy Spirit and develop the kind of intimacy that only comes from spending much time with Him will lead us into many extraordinary places. By letting Him do the speaking most of the time, He has ordered my own steps into many interesting experiences. On one occasion I was out late walking, spending time meditating on the Word and just being quiet, while listening to what the Holy Spirit would say. He reminded me of the many times through answers to prayer and other very personal experiences when He revealed how He had been leading my life. It was as if He was showing images from, *"This Is Your Life"*, except He was doing the directing, each time pointing out the wisdom of the Father. After the Holy Spirit had outlined and highlighted for me all of these experiences, He told me, "I want you to share these moments with other believers in church on Wednesday night." I told Him immediately, "I am not going to do that." (It just seemed too personal and at first I was unwilling to unveil this to others.)

Most of my life I had been a private person, so when I did speak I felt it was worth expressing, though many times it seemed that not everyone would take me seriously. The Holy Spirit was still insistent about me sharing on that Wednesday night church service. I told Him, "Alright, I will share, but I am not coming into that meeting, barging in as though I had something to say. You will have to open a way, or I won't say anything."

Wednesday night came around and I went to the church service, which met in the pastor's home. The evening started out like numerous other times, in prayer and worship. The pastor's wife, Lori, was leading it. While we were singing, suddenly she stopped playing the guitar and spoke these words, "There is someone here to whom the Holy Spirit has already spoken to share some things. You just need to speak and trust the Lord." Now the Holy Spirit had my mail. He knew my heart, and He knew how to make a way that was consistent with what I had asked Him.

We sat in the living-room of their home. It was completely silent when I began speaking about all those intimate times the Holy Spirit had reminded me of just a couple of days before the meeting. As I was sharing, He started speaking in my inner-man. He told me, *"You are releasing life into this room!"* The words that I was saying were bringing life to that room. They were filled with His glory, very intimate in everything I said. He was doing the orchestrating this time. I continued through eyes that were wet with tears, speaking as He was leading me. There was a woman sitting in the chair right in front of my seat, and she knew inside her that she felt some change. She was being healed and exclaimed that something was happening to her then. She and Lori left the room so that she could privately examine what she felt had taken place.

Another individual (this was Matt's very first time in this church) was so moved by the power of God and the intimacy created by the Holy Spirit, that he said, "I just need to give my life to Jesus right now!" There was no altar call; there was no sermon preached. It was the pure, sincere word by the Holy Spirit that was being released in that room, as the Lord had spoken to me, *"You are releasing life into this room."* When Lori and the other lady came back into the room, both of them were ecstatic. This woman had gone to the doctor's office earlier in the day. The doctor had discovered a lump on her breast and diagnosed it as cancerous. At first, during the prayer meeting, the lump had been disappearing, but when the two women examined further, it was completely gone. She had been healed!

He knew how to set the stage. He sees the end from the beginning. He just wanted us to be able to participate with Him. We are learning to follow the voice of the Holy Spirit, learning to just trust His leading even if it seems uncomfortable to us. He delights in all our experiences that come up higher in Him, experiencing intimately all that the Father has intended for all of our lives.

That young man, Matt, had given his life to Jesus that night. He is now a pastor of a church in Oregon. We never know all that is on the Father's heart and mind, but we do know what He reveals to us will supernaturally change the surroundings. The nature of the words that Jesus spoke are recorded by John as, "It is the Spirit who gives life; the flesh profits nothing. The words that I speak to you are spirit, and they are life" (John 6:63 NKJV). We can say with all confidence, "The words I say, they are spirit and they are life!" That is what the Holy Spirit reminded me while I was speaking in that service. He continues to guide and teach us so that it would not be missed what His glory tastes like, and how it is being manifested through us.

Riches of Glory

8

Training Wheels

A ll that may be deemed as chaos in the universe is by His appointment, not by Him creating it that way. He has chosen that we would work with Him by His own sovereign choice and authority. The chaos is the transitory condition set before us so that we should willingly use our faith to stand in His favor, rejoicing, knowing His glory changes all things, restoring the order already declared by Him. "Declaring the end from the beginning, and from ancient times things that are not yet done, saying, 'My counsel shall stand, and I will do all My pleasure'" (Isaiah 46:10 NKJV). This rich truth is unveiled by the Holy Spirit for us to see the end from the beginning. We see in that spiritual realm the end results.

Seeing the truth as real because He said it, in spite of what our eyes see or our ears hear, is the ground that we stand on confidently. It becomes a deliberate action on our part to speak words which are in alignment with His words. When we stream with Him in His glory, we taste what His glory is like in our mouths. This experiential knowing, this intimately knowing, is exactly what is meant by "the knowledge of the glory". Our spirit is aligned with His Spirit. That alignment is called obedience to the faith, following the voice of the Holy Spirit. We are thankful that He has given us the Holy Spirit. We are thankful to truly know the voice of the Holy Spirit. The signs mean more to the Holy Spirit's wisdom concerning things we do not know ourselves. We just trust the Holy Spirit and yield ourselves to following His voice. We obey His voice, even though it is this still small voice in our spirit. We become accustomed to knowing His voice through daily spending time with the Father. This walk for us is one that develops as we follow the voice of the Holy Spirit—obedience to the faith.

Faith works within us like training wheels on a bike. We ride with greater ease when first starting out because of those training wheels. Faith accompanies not only our early steps as a believer, but now since we have an understanding of how faith works, we can step more easily and deliberately into this realm of His glory. Faith helps set that direction and deliberateness in our spirit, so that we can stand in His favor and know exactly what and how something will manifest through our spoken words. It helps to keep us humble, especially while expressing these simple truths to others who are just now being awakened, when we remember where we have come from and how some situations seemed difficult to us at first.

After working all night at my job, I hurriedly ran to the bus stop to make the connections that would take me to the transfer stop then on to where I lived in a townhouse. It was payday Friday and I wanted to be able to cash my check right away because I had already made plans for the weekend. Normally, I would not have had any thought about rushing to have cash on hand but simply waited for a more convenient time. When I reached my stop on the route, it was still too early since the bank lobby would not be open for another two hours. The night shift was starting to catch up with me, so I was thinking more about sleep than cashing my check; however, knowing my own habits, I did not want to oversleep and miss all business hours at the bank.

I made a decision that even though I did not want to stay up any longer, I would at least get personal business out of the way, so I stepped inside a nearby craft store in the interim as I waited for the bank to open. While I was in the store, I had a casual conversation with the owner about what I was waiting on and if I could look around. He offered that the drive-up window would be open in about ten minutes; I would not have to wait for the branch to open. I liked that idea, so I quickly left the store and stood with the cars at the drive-thru window. I had been walking up closer to the window as each customer finished their business. After the guy on the motorcycle in front of me I would finally be next.

When it was my turn, I told the clerk right away that I only wanted to cash my payroll check. She said that she could not do that because I was on foot; the window only served drive-up customers. I inquired about the previous customer being on a motorcycle. Her answer was that the insurance didn't cover any pedestrians but only moving transportation.

The end result—I was denied the privilege of cashing my check early in the morning as I had planned. I made a decision right then that no matter what I would get my check cashed and at the same window of the same clerk who had told me as long as I was a pedestrian I would not be able.

You know this tenacious attitude has to be tempered, but it is also the type of passion that we need to have alive in our hearts over every single promise of God—that we will not be denied. We are not getting the Father to do anything that He had not already sovereignly authorized by covenant. All of His promises are *yes* in Christ. More precisely, we are activating our faith in the promise, knowing already what we expect the end result to be. "For all the promises of God in Him are Yes, and in Him Amen, to the glory of God through us" (2 Corinthians 1:20 NKJV).

Sleep did not matter now, I was on a mission (I think it energized me more because of it.) As I walked back towards my place I saw a bicycle repair shop. Instantly I had an inspirational idea. I stopped and talked with the owner of this shop. I told him what it was that I wanted to accomplish and what it required for me to use the drive-up window. I asked him if I might borrow one of his bikes to ride over to the bank drive-up window to cash my check, then I would promptly return his bike when finished. He was hesitant to let anything leave his shop because of past problems of theft in the area. I assured him that I only had one goal and that my word was good. Still, I could tell he needed a little more persuasion, so I offered my employee id as collateral since it was required for entry into the building. When I added a twenty dollar bill as a deposit, he finally conceded and picked out a bicycle for me.

I left the bicycle repair shop with a borrowed bike that had cost me collateral, my employee id, plus a twenty dollar bill. This was a little girl's bike, something you would give to your daughter who was not quite in second grade. I might also mention, I would have never given this bike to either of my daughters or anyone else's daughter for that matter. It was so rickety that the front tire wobbled back and forth making it very difficult to steer. My knees were up in my chest while trying to peddle this contraption, but I was no longer a pedestrian! (I think I might have had a smirk on my face, thinking about the expression on the clerk's face as I rode up on my new wheels.)

I rode right up to the customer lane that I had been in that morning. This time I was prepared. Straddled over the little girl's bike, I politely requested to have my check cashed. The window clerk said absolutely nothing. It was all business, a straight forward mannerism. I did not break character, even when I could see a couple of the bank managers through the window in the background laughing hysterically. She meticulously counted out each bill as I watched and listened. I confirmed the amount and placed it in my wallet. With my head held high, I peddled out of the parking lot on the back of this two-wheeled motor-less vehicle. I had accomplished what I set out to do. Of course, I returned this work of art and exchanged it for my employee id and twenty dollar deposit.

Riches of Glory

9

Don't Eat the Grass

*F*ool's Gold Christianity is a phrase I have coined which describes the types of experiences found within the church today. What could be understood by the use of this phrase? There are types of Christians today who truly do have a born-again experience, but in their ability to be discipled there are myriads of examples that prove they only have a form of godliness, but deny the power. All that glitters is not gold. Even though it is weighty, it may only be lead and not gold. Proverbs 25:2 gives us the Father's wisdom on this, "*It is* the glory of God to conceal a matter, but the glory of kings *is* to search out a matter."

What God has concealed by covenant design, He has promised to reveal but with His discretionary purpose and choice. The singular path Jesus spoke about is two-fold: No one comes to the Father except through Jesus. And unless the Father draws you, no one comes to Christ. The whole realm of His glory is only concealed from fair-weather believers, but those who truly taste pure glory wisdom are never the same again. Everything has changed in their lives. The knowledge of the glory has become permanent residency in their innermost being. In John 15:7, Jesus said it this way, "If you abide in Me, and My words abide in you, you will ask whatever you will, and it will be done for you." The word "abide" is the permanent residency of His word.

The images that are so common to most Christians become revelatory wisdom to unveil more of this knowledge of the glory of the Lord. For example when Peter walked on water, he asked the Lord Jesus by faith if that was Him he saw walking on water, "Lord, if that is You, bid me to come to You on the water." Jesus said one word that was supersaturated with His glory, "Come." That word empowered Peter to walk on water. Peter received that ability from Jesus; however, it did not yet have permanent residency within him. Jesus never needed to have His mind renewed. We do. The comparison between Peter's and Jesus' experiences reveals that one walked by faith and the other walked by glory. Glory wisdom comes in higher than everything else.

We have not yet even understood that there *is* the gospel of the glory, let alone that this *was* sound doctrine all along (1 Timothy 1:11). Of special note, it is very interesting that the whole purpose of the gospel is for obtaining the glory of the Lord Jesus Christ (2 Thessalonians 2:14). Is this taught on a regular basis with any consistency that establishes every new believer? These simple truths are for building every one of us from only a believer to becoming a disciple. We are to become so well acquainted with His glory that we do not follow any other voice, only the voice of the Holy Spirit. Do you want fool's gold or the real thing? Every miracle that Jesus performed, He did because the Father was in Him, and He was in the Father. That heavenly model is exactly what we step into at the beginning through communion to activate His glory within us. He abides in me, and I abide in Him.

Now that the Father has access to us through covenant, our steps are ordered by Him. We become aware of it more through accessing the new nature within us. Perfect peace is the reality of our new nature. The Holy Spirit teaches us to work with Him in the operation of laser light surgery — sanctification. We can tell the difference between the old nature and the new nature; we can discern between ripples on the pond and perfect peace. Mostly what has been taught is that we should try to be more like Christ, but Christ is already like Christ. When Jesus was walking on water, He was walking in Christ, walking in the glory. When Peter was walking on water, he was walking in Peter, empowered by the glory that was released from what Jesus spoke.

The sign says, **DON'T EAT THE GRASS**. We are His sheep, and we see the sign, but sheep cannot read the signs. So given enough time the sheep will knock the sign down and eat it. The Shepherd knows the wisdom for the sign and also knows His sheep. He sees them eating the grass and immediately leads them to better and higher pasture. The sheep follow the Shepherd's voice; the voice of a stranger they do not follow.

The wisdom that the Shepherd had concerning the grass in my illustration is that He knew already the grass was toxic and that it was harmful to the sheep. He also knew there was nothing wrong with the sign. It displayed the truth perfectly concerning what was good and acceptable for the benefit of the sheep, and as the true Shepherd, Jesus knew what must be done.

Jesus Himself fulfilled the sign that reads: *All the commandments are fulfilled in Christ.* Now to have wisdom concerning Christ, you must know what went into the Bread of Life recipe. Whatever went into Heaven's recipe is now in you, because Christ is in you. This is in Christ—ALL THE LAW AND PROPHETS ARE FULFILLED. He never lied, so when He said, "It is finished", that is exactly what happened on our behalf. It is a deception from the enemy to draw our attention to anything less than that or distract from what has already been fulfilled in Christ. The reality is truly known when we understand the knowledge of the glory more precisely. It unveils all truth concerning Christ in us—the hope of glory.

Consider carefully another illustration: I am giving to you my exact pizza recipe and the *exact law,* which are the directions and instructions on how to make it, along with the exact ingredients and proportions. If your pizza does not turn out the same as mine, you have just fallen short of the *glory* of how good my pizza truly is. I am the owner and creator of my own recipe. Now, when I make my own recipe for you, I *fulfill* all the instructions on how to make it. I use the exact ingredients and proportions, so it is not necessary for you to fulfill it. I have already made it, now it is your turn. When I am in your kitchen and you follow my voice exactly, you are making the pizza exactly how I make it. I am leading and guiding you to make my pizza perfectly. Now, when you trust my voice on what I say, even if you have never made my pizza before, it will turn out perfectly, because I know exactly how to make it.

I had created a contest for all of my kids when they were younger to compete making their best dish in the kitchen—a *bake off*. They were each given a different family recipe and were going to make something that they had never made before (this was before the days of "MasterChef Junior".) I had chosen which recipes I wanted each of them to produce. My mom and I supervised while they were all allowed to use their own abilities in getting the ingredients, bowls, mixers, etc., together.

Flour was everywhere: on the counters, table, and floor. Anywhere there was a surface, flour or sugar covered it. The nature of leading others means adjusting to the messiness. We have to be willing for them to spill things and make a mess. The focus is not on the process of what or how but actually on the end results—the things being made. Initially, we take our own skills and tempering by the Holy Spirit to lead others in ministry or prayer, until they have developed the ability to fine-tune their own skills to hear and follow the voice of the Holy Spirit.

The contest that I set in motion with my children, immediately engaged their interests. They all wanted to do their best. They were very excited to make their own creations that would come out of the kitchen. The decision to back off and allow them to do everything on their own from start to finish released me from having to perfect anything for them. They were given the helm and I would just oversee to help direct. Their experience would be their own accomplishment rather than to watch dad make something and enjoy the results from what I might produce. I gave Joel my famous pizza recipe to make from scratch, which included the recipe for both the dough and the sauce. He is the oldest so I felt assured he was suited for the task. Although, an oversight occurred on my part because I was busy taking note of the progress of the others; Joel had used cold water when he added yeast. It took a lot longer to rise, but by providing a little heat to the dough, it was at least usable. When the hot pizza came out of the oven, it was superb in flavor!

April was given the opportunity to make her grand-mother's fabulous pie dough. She made personalized marionberry pies, since each child's finished dish would be tasted by everyone. That way we became our own judges over each child's results coupled by accountability with one another. Daniel made my dad's delicious chocolate fudge recipe, which takes a refined skill to make. His masterpiece was perfect with my direct coaching. In my first book, *"Glory Revealed"*, I told the story about the time my daughters had their first experience making this family fudge recipe. Theirs had fallen short of the goal they had in mind.

Candice, being the youngest and only six at the time, was given the simple recipe for making chocolate chip cookies. Although, without any understanding or experience, no recipe will turn out correctly on the first attempt. She had the privilege of making cookies with others before, so this would be something she was a little more familiar with. The difference now, she would create the cookie dough all on her own. For the task of baking things and anything that involved using the oven, I took deliberate charge and the liberty to ensure the safety and handling of things going in and out of the oven.

The culinary skills that they enjoyed on that particular day helped develop many things, on many levels, especially in gaining confidence that they could make things on their own. This was not their first time being in the kitchen. Many times in the past they would watch or help with little things at first. Once while their grandma was canning apricots, and then placing the sealed jars on a cutting board, Joel, being very inquisitive, had asked his grandma what she was making. She told him that she was canning apricots. He asked her, "Are there *joelcots*?" (He was mindful of his sister, April.) I think because he heard the word *apricots* and felt that he was just as important, there should also be something named after him, *joelcots*. That is something the Father is trying to get us to understand, our identity in Christ makes us just as important as Christ. It is why we have the same glory, the same faith, and the same love. We are ONE!

Riches of Glory

10

Perfect Vessels

G race empowers us to STAND, not fall. When we stand, therefore, we can rejoice with Him, and His glory is manifested in all we say and do. We are walking in the light *effortlessly. I am the righteousness of God in Christ;* this is present tense. It is the nature of the new creation, the nature of Christ, and the nature of His glory. The old nature has only one purpose from the Father —it must die. We do not prune it, form it, try to make it better, or try to perfect it. The old nature must die. That is the Father's only answer for the old nature. We have two natures now: the old nature and the new nature. We are training the mind to respond to the new nature by fine-tuning the mind to know and understand the voice of the Holy Spirit.

His glory in us is ever-increasing. Do you believe this? He said that we would walk in greater works. Is there a limit or boundary on those greater works? The glory of the Father is the glory which Jesus has given us. The Holy Spirit has made it His priority to train us on how to operate with ever increasing wisdom and revelation concerning His glory. We can read in 2 Corinthians 4:17 that the glory is "an eternal weight of glory." It is immeasurable! There is absolutely nothing that any of us are presently facing that His glory does not outweigh. It outshines anything that this world has to offer either in riches or in suffering. His glory is always greater. What is not factored into this equation adequately is that we do not have revelation without the Holy Spirit, who trains us in how to partner and partake of His divine nature. Thank you Father for sending Your Holy Spirit!

Each day, become so acquainted with the voice of the Holy Spirit that each word He speaks resonates within you and sets you free to partake more of His glory. You should have total and complete peace over each and every degree of suffering that you will encounter in this world. That should so ignite your joy inside you that you have more glory available today than you did yesterday. His presence overshadows us, not by our minds understanding, but by our spirits receiving. Our minds do not have the capacity to absolutely comprehend all things until His glory is being released by experience. Consider what this might taste like: *nothing is impossible*. Do you believe this? It is the work of the Holy Spirit to make this revelation a reality in your spirit-man. That *nothing is impossible* quality of His glory will show up on your lips. It will be noticed in your words. His glory has become one with your person. Every day you can test this and know that what I am declaring is absolutely the truth. Amen!

We fine-tune the mind by attentively listening to the voice of the Holy Spirit. By constant practice, the mind, which still has access to the old nature, is now being trained and tutored by the Holy Spirit to be very clear in discerning with precise wisdom regarding anything, concerning any condition set before us. His wisdom becomes fused with our thoughts. It empowers us to accurately discern. Be replenished in Him! Without being filled with Him we have nothing to give. We tune in to the Holy Spirit, to fine-tune our view on our surroundings and we transform our minds so that our world around us conforms to Him.

The language of the Father is creative language. The words He speaks are what transforms and creates. Our minds need transforming. Jesus has given us *mind-transforming* exercises to engage with by saying these words, "The words I speak are spirit and life." Notice when you first say these words (while looking in the mirror), they are not perceived as being true. It is only proving one thing: your mind is not renewed as yet. This is the reason Jesus said, "Abide in My word."

We should also take note what He spoke concerning communion, "As often as you do this, do in remembrance of Me." We are to *remind our minds that Christ is in us manifesting His glory*. His creative nature is perfused through every cell of our being, so that we are permeated and saturated with His glory. Our whole being is inundated with Christ. "As often as you do this," (the language of communion) reminds our mind that we are completely immersed with Christ. That is our new nature, which is taking direction from the Holy Spirit and coming into alignment with how the Father thinks. The Holy Spirit has to convince us that we are the *righteousness of God in Christ!*

The words that come from the Holy Spirit absolutely empower us. They are creative and miraculous words that come from the Father of glory who is sitting on the Throne of Glory; therefore, every word that the Holy Spirit speaks to us is a word that comes from the Throne of Glory. No other wisdom comes in as high as the wisdom, the revelation, and the knowledge of the glory. The Word that came from the Father of glory is life; it empowers, uplifts, and rearranges, because His word is creative, energized, and full of power. His glory is released through us in word form, through the exact words that we speak and declare. This is the living reality of what the treasure is like in us that Jesus described. "A good man out of the good treasure of his heart brings forth good things, and an evil man out of the evil treasure brings forth evil things" (Matthew 12:35 NKJV).

What Jesus speaks is full of life; His words transform and energize. His glory is one with His word; it ignites within you and radiates. Fanning this flame inside you causes it to rise up and out of your mouth. Your words now have the same glory and authority when they are spoken. They are fused with His glory. Jesus operated in the same glory, and said that apart from the Father, He could do nothing. Now apart from Him you can do nothing. Your words have become one with His glory, so you do not necessarily have to memorize Scripture anymore, which is the foundation; but because your understanding of the Word and your relationship with the Holy Spirit go much deeper. You are in reality speaking what the Holy Spirit speaks. His glory, together with your words, is capable of doing anything imaginable.

We are perfect vessels already and only need to yield to Him to be useful for every good work. That word *work* is elusive, for if it is viewed from man's perspective, it carries a meaning that there is something we can do that originates with us and done in our own strength. Even though we do something that seems to have religious value, it is only a form of godliness but denies the power. When Jesus commanded, either believe the words I say or the works I do, those works He referred to are supernatural works. They are manifestations of His glory, works that the Father Himself was doing through Him.

In Ephesians, we read, "Stand in the power of His might." Even in standing, it is done in Him with His glory. The works that we do are works that are ONLY manifestations of His glory, works that are ONLY being led by the Holy Spirit in us. In truth, it can be said "...from glory to glory." It is His glory which initiated; it is His glory which formed and founded the work; and it is His glory which manifests and finishes the work. It is truly the Father of glory in us doing the work. This is the glory Jesus has received, and this is the glory He gave us. Our choice to yield to the Holy Spirit places us in this glory stream, which is completely the work of the Father in, on, and all around us. NOTHING is done on our part, except to be the willing vessels of honor—vessels of glory—to which He has chosen and appointed us by His own creative authority.

Without a doubt, those who hear the voice of the Holy Spirit and are yielded to Him, talk more love than anything else. This is how He calls us, sends us, protects us, and empowers us—by His love. Jesus said that He loved us first. He has chosen us and appointed us. That appointment is the commissioning, which has given us everything that He has. This is how He prays: in the same way that the Father has sent Him, we too, would be sent. We are sent in the fullness of His glory. We are being tutored privately, very personally by the Holy Spirit, who only speaks words from the Throne of Glory. Everything that the Holy Spirit teaches is this knowledge of the glory, so that we are not only receiving the wisdom and revelation of His glory, but with every morsel, we are being empowered to work and operate with Him in His glory—from glory to glory.

The enemy cannot change our wills, but he can have access to our tongue if it is unruly and does not align with what the Word declares about any condition that is set before us. It is the tongue that has the power of life and death. We must love the fruit that comes from the Holy Spirit when our tongues are yielded to His service. This is how we present ourselves before our minds are transformed; we present and surrender our spirit to Him in spiritual worship. We present all the members of our body as well.

Death and life are in the power of the tongue, and those who love it will eat its fruit. (Proverbs 18:21 NKJV)

Therefore, I urge you, brothers and sisters, in view of God's mercy, to offer your bodies as a living sacrifice, holy and pleasing to God—this is your true and proper worship. Do not conform to the pattern of this world, but be transformed by the renewing of your mind. Then you will be able to test and approve what God's will is—His good, pleasing and perfect will. (Romans 12:1, 2 NIV)

11

Invasion of Peace

*L*et's review the words of Jesus' prayer in John, chapter 17, "Father, I desire that they also whom You gave Me may be with Me where I am, that they may behold My glory which You have given Me; for You loved Me before the foundation of the world" (John 17:24 NKJV). There are a few things that should be noted in verse 24. He had been proclaiming in previous verses, that He wanted us to be One, and the way He was going to do this was by giving us the glory. He then prays His desires that we would be perfected in the glory. Now, looking directly at verse 24, the prerequisites were those words He previously prayed, which positioned us to receive His *greatest* desire for us. Verse 24 reveals the depth of the Father's heart, His desire for us; and that the plans He has for us to operate in His glory have existed since before He created anything else. This had always been Jesus' desire for us—one with Him and the Father—operating in His glory from the throne.

Why has the enemy blinded many from understanding *"The Gospel of the Glory"?* Because he has seen and felt the implications of the Glory that has been activated and is radiating out of the lives of believers. These weapons that we possess are extremely powerful when compared to anything that the enemy may appear to have. When we understand how to effectively walk in this wisdom, *the knowledge of the Glory,* then it thwarts, impedes, and utterly destroys the enemy's plans in every endeavor he may try to launch. He uses deceit and craftiness when expressing any Bible verse, things that sound true to the untrained mind and the untuned ear. Our hearts and minds are guarded by Jesus' peace in us (an overflow indicator of His glory that is activated in us).

"Be still, and know that I am God; I will be exalted among the nations, I will be exalted in the earth!" (Psalm 46:10 NKJV). We've often heard people using the beginning part of this verse, but it is doubtful that the timing of when to be still is understood. This verse comes right on the heels of the Father revealing the tremendous display of power and authority on our behalf, in verses 8 and 9, "Come, behold the works of the Lord, who has made desolations in the earth. He makes wars cease to the end of the earth; He breaks the bow and cuts the spear in two; He burns the chariot in the fire" (Psalm 46:8, 9 NKJV). One of the ways in which His glory operates is to end wars for us, bringing peace through the entire realm! We behold His works and watch wars cease by His power. That is the kind of Glory that the Father has. The Father and His Glory are one. Jesus received the Glory of the Father. Jesus gave this Glory to you and me.

We use this *flavor* of His glory, this wisdom and knowledge of the glory to bring peace wherever the Holy Spirit leads us.

You must know that Father God is deeply interested in the affairs of your country to protect the people's interests and set an example to all free people around the world. We have the voice of the Lion of the tribe of Judah standing and supporting those who have made a breakthrough. David, in the Bible, made such a breakthrough, and then all those with him were encouraged to push out opposing forces. The Father is with us, and He is well able to defeat all of our enemies. The enemy, satan, always stirs up strife and creates confusion as he tries to be the center of attention; however, we know that Jesus has already made us more than conquerors. Wrestle with the principalities and powers in the spiritual realm to establish His glory throughout your land! It is our covenant privilege to lift up our voice in one accord, praying, expecting, and knowing that He has deposited His glory in us for such a time as this.

Thank you Father, that You have given such favor and wisdom to all those who are called by Your name. We thank You for revealing the truth that Your glory in us is the very same glory operating in Jesus our Lord. Today, we agree, with all of our brothers and sisters across the land, to stand in the gap for all of Your people, and we believe that You will mightily move on their behalf according to Your wisdom and word; "Come, behold the works of the Lord, Who has made desolations in the earth. He makes wars cease to the end of the earth; He breaks the bow and cuts the spear in two. He burns the chariot in the fire.

Be still, and know that I am God; I will be exalted among the nations, I will be exalted in the earth!" (Psalm 46:8-10)

His reputation and His honor are what is being accounted to us. All the accolades, all that Jesus achieved on the cross, and all that the Father bestowed on Him when the Glory of the Father raised Christ from the dead—we have received as well. This is what we inherited when we received His glory. The greatest victory that He achieved is the resurrection from the grave. That victory is inherent in the New Creation, which is the supernatural nature within us.

The kingdom is first established in us then manifested through us. It began in seed form when the Holy Spirit spoke to us and was received in our hearts. It activates in us and radiates from us when we begin speaking in alignment with Him. The Father jealously guards what He has entrusted to us. The word that is activated in us, which came first to us by the Holy Spirit, has all of His divine protection with it. It is important to Him; therefore, it is important to us. He expects that we guard our hearts and minds with this same deliberateness.

We have heard before that the sword we hold, the sword of the Spirit, is a double-edged sword. There is blessing and there is cursing in this sword. We have divine protection both defensively and offensively. We only need to stand on any one of His promises. That is an operation we do in the spirit; however, we have a New Covenant, and it is the language of the New Covenant that the Father jealously protects, honors, and faithfully administers to His children—the children of light.

His covenant names throughout Scripture were how the children of Israel understood and experienced the nature of the covenant that was revealed to them in their empiricism. They knew Him as YHWH, which are the four Hebrew consonants that represent His name: Yod, He, Vav, He. There are many combinations of this word in which other words are added to reveal yet another aspect true to His nature, for instance Jehovah-Jireh, and Jehovah-Rophe. Their meanings: I am the God who provides, and I am the God who heals, respectively.

Jesus reveals the nature of the Father by saying, "I Am." He reveals the unique relationship that He has with the Father. The New Covenant is first established with us in our relationship with Jesus, and then it is established with us and the Father. He who has the Son has the Father also (1 John 2:23). It is extremely important to understand the uniqueness we have in our relationship with the Father. The following combinations that we have in the New Covenant reveal the nature of the Father: Father of glory, Father of spirits, and Father of lights. All of these phrases are the one true God. We are receiving from Him the manifold wisdom that enables and empowers us to fully work with Him in His glory.

The language in these verses is very specific, unveiling more of the hidden mysteries and treasures concerning His glory. Jesus calls God, His Father. This brought about much of the disharmony and discord from among the Jews, for they understood that if God were His Father, then Jesus would be equal to God. What is it that makes us equal with Jesus? "For it was fitting for Him, for whom are all things and by whom are all things, in bringing many sons to glory, to make the captain of their salvation perfect through sufferings. For both He who sanctifies and those who are being sanctified are all of one, for which reason He is not ashamed to call them brethren" (Hebrews 2:10, 11 NKJV). When we are crying or feeling any other kind of hurt, it is truly Him in us also crying. These expressions reveal how intimate our relationship with the Father is that we genuinely have. He is not just sympathetic with our suffering, He is one with our suffering in the exact way that we are experiencing.

Christ sanctified Himself, so that we are also sanctified. That word's root meaning is *to set apart.* He is in us; consequently, we are set apart, not by our choosing, but by the work of the Holy Spirit. The purpose for setting us apart is to make known the mysteries that are hidden in Christ but now are being revealed in us. A better way to understand this is by comparing in the Word phrases like "all-consuming fire", "God is light", and "fan into flame the gift of God within you". This can be easily understood when Christ enters your life and sets you apart; your life turns to flame and you are being transformed. That word that came by revelation from the Holy Spirit is what was imparted to you. A different direction to see the same truth is this: if God were *absolute zero*, when Christ shows up and enters our lives, we would all be frozen.

We are imparting His nature when we lay hands on anyone or speak His words. "If you abide in Me, and My words abide in you, you will ask what you desire, and it shall be done for you" (John 15:7 NKJV). "Peter said, 'Silver and gold I do not have, but what I do have I give you: In the name of Jesus Christ of Nazareth, rise up and walk'" (Acts 3:6 NKJV). What you possess, you give. If you do not own it, then you have nothing to give.

It is important that we possess what the Holy Spirit reveals. He may reveal, yet we do not possess it until it has been released through our words and our works. Jesus said, *either believe the words I say, or believe the works I do.* His nature in us is the same, either believe the words we say, or the works we do. We first fill up on what the Holy Spirit has revealed, and then by walking that out we possess it. We engage this each time we release His glory to others by acknowledging that what we have is what we give.

Hear the words that Jesus said, "Now I am no longer in the world, but these are in the world, and I come to You. Holy Father, keep through Your name those whom You have given Me, that they may be one as We are" (John 17:11 NKJV). He is speaking with the same veracity with which we speak concerning being seated with Him in heavenly places. We should be able to exercise our faith by using His Word to say, "I am no longer in this world. I am seated in heavenly places in Christ!"

I might add that within this same verse, notice that He does not say we *may be one*, but He says, *"...be one as We are."* Now if the Father and Jesus were zebras and spoke this to us we would get this completely. That you may be one like us is exactly what He is saying. We are like Him in authority, faith, love, power, and glory. This is the hope that John spoke of in one of his letters; "Beloved, now we are children of God; and it has not yet been revealed what we shall be, but we know that when He is revealed, we shall be like Him, for we shall see Him as He is. And everyone who has this hope in Him purifies himself, just as He is pure" (1 John 3:2, 3 NKJV). And again within this same letter, "Love has been perfected among us in this: that we may have boldness in the day of judgment; because as He is, so are we in this world" (1 John 4:17 NKJV).

We are not like Him on our own, but we are like Him because the Holy Spirit in us has sealed our true selves in Christ. That is the image we are conformed to. Whatever gets revealed by the Holy Spirit, which is just one more promise from the Father, is what gets highlighted in our lives, so that we partake of His divine nature. Without Christ, we are still just living from our old nature; the new nature would not even be known. In Christ we are new creations by the Father's purpose and design. In Christ all that is true of the new creation is true in us. We can gain true insight and revelation from the Holy Spirit by knowing what this new creation is like, by directly seeing how this new creation is operating in Christ. "...as He is so are we in this world".

12

You Are Loved and Not Forgotten

*T*he phrase *washing of water* found in Ephesians is very interesting to consider because of how clean He makes us through the Word that comes to us by the Holy Spirit. "That He might sanctify and cleanse her with the washing of water by the word" (Ephesians 5:26 NKJV) He makes us clean through the word that comes to us by the Holy Spirit. He washes the water, cleanses it, so that the water cleans us. He does this by His spoken word. The words He speaks are so pure and holy that they transform our thinking by those words being received. I asked my daughter, April, this question to draw out from her how one would make chocolate milk white again? Her immediate answer, "You keep pouring white milk 'til the chocolate milk is white again." Jesus washes all the chocolate milk out of us, so that we crave the sincere, pure milk of the word.

The purity of His words proves that the glory manifested is the signature from the Father that says we have come into alignment with Him. His truth always manifests His glory. Until we actually connect this heavenly model—I in you and you in Me—that alignment is not known by others. He is perfecting in us what He had deposited. That perfecting comes in the form of relationship, knowing the Father loves me in the same way that the Father loves the Son. You are empowered to boldly declare whatever you will. You are validated by the Father Himself. He qualified you already to work with Him in His glory. Thank you Father, wake up Your glory!

When He is speaking about *"the knowledge of the glory"*, He has already purposed in His heart that this is an intimate experiential knowledge. You have complete understanding in the very truth that He establishes within you. You have transitioned in your thinking from a wondering state to a knowing state. Deliberately exercise your will to choose to only do what you see the Holy Spirit doing, and to only say what you hear the Holy Spirit saying. This same condition was brought out in Jesus' own words, *I only do what I see the Father doing. I only say what I hear the Father saying.* The truth being established in you is that you are tasting and seeing His glory. Your sensitivity to distinguish the voice of the Holy Spirit is what has been perfected through constant use and consistent practice. In Him we live and move and have our being!

Therefore the Jews sought all the more to kill Him, because He not only broke the Sabbath, but also said that God was His Father, making Himself equal with God. Then Jesus answered and said to them, "Most assuredly, I say to you, the Son can do nothing of Himself, but what He sees the Father do; for whatever He does, the Son also does in like manner. For the Father loves the Son, and shows Him all things that He Himself does; and He will show Him greater works than these, that you may marvel. For as the Father raises the dead and gives life to them, even so the Son gives life to whom He will. For the Father judges no one, but has committed all judgment to the Son, that all should honor the Son just as they honor the Father. He who does not honor the Son does not honor the Father who sent Him. (John 5:18-23 NKJV)

In John, chapter 5, Jesus said He could do nothing on His own, but only what He saw the Father doing. The significance of these words deeply reflects on our relationship that He has given to us by the Holy Spirit who is in us. These words set in motion the language of ONE founded in the New Covenant. We only do what we see the Holy Spirit doing. He is only leading us from that which Jesus has received. This alignment in the spirit realm accurately defines the wisdom of the Father's glory in us.

If we follow the words of Jesus, we see that the *greater works* are manifested through us by the relationship (between the Father and Jesus) which has already been founded on Love. The strength of knowing His Love in us and for us makes us free in the spiritual realm that Jesus is unveiling to us by the wisdom from the Father. The Father is not holding back one thing from us. He is revealing all things that He does. This genuineness of the truth is established by Jesus' own character. It is expressed from His heart in the prayer recorded in John, chapter 17. "I in them, and You in Me; that they may be made perfect in one, and that the world may know that You have sent Me, and have loved them as You have loved Me. And I have declared to them Your name, and will declare it, that the love with which You loved Me may be in them, and I in them" (John 17:23, 26 NKJV).

The Father of glory as He is called is found in Ephesians, "That the God of our Lord Jesus Christ, the Father of glory, may give to you the spirit of wisdom and revelation in the knowledge of Him" (Ephesians 1:17 NKJV).

James writes, "Every good gift and every perfect gift is from above, and comes down from the Father of lights, with whom there is no variation or shadow of turning" (James 1:17 NKJV).

And finally, in Hebrews, "Furthermore, we have had human fathers who corrected us, and we paid them respect. Shall we not much more readily be in subjection to the Father of spirits and live?" (Hebrews 12:9 NKJV).

The Father has qualified us and established us through His Love for us and in us. We now have direct access to this kingdom of light. "For through Him we both have access by one Spirit to the Father" (Ephesians 2:18 NKJV). "In whom we have boldness and access with confidence through faith in Him" (Ephesians 3:12 NKJV). "Giving thanks to the Father who has qualified us to be partakers of the inheritance of the saints in the light. He has delivered us from the power of darkness and conveyed us into the kingdom of the Son of His love" (Colossians 1:12, 13 NKJV).

Why is light given to him who is in misery, and life to the bitter of soul? (Job 3:20 NKJV)

To bring back his soul from the Pit, that he may be enlightened with the light of life. (Job 33:30 NKJV)

In Him was life, and the life was the light of men. And the light shines in the darkness, and the darkness did not comprehend it. (John 1:4, 5 NKJV).

The covenant of Love is expressed in the relationship we have in marriage and is a reflection of the Father's heart. It is because of this intimate relationship established by the Father that it has been under much attack by the enemy, resulting with many marriages ending in divorce which plagues our society throughout. We enter into temptation with the enemy due to a lack of genuine experiences in Christ and truly knowing the benefits of walking steadfastly in covenant relationship with the Father.

"The relationship with the Father is so intimate it feels like us." The Holy Spirit spoke to me once over a question I had posed to the Father concerning this verse, "But we have this treasure in jars of clay to show that this all-surpassing power is from God and not from us" (2 Corinthians 4:7 NIV). After meditating on it, I had asked Him, "Why would You even write this in the Bible? We already know this all-surpassing power is from You and not ourselves."

Today, say with your heart these words, "How can I bless You, Holy Father? You have deposited Your glory in me. You have qualified me to enjoy Your kingdom of light. You have chosen to conform me to the image of Your Son, as a son of glory." Jesus said, "… as you have done it to the least of these my brethren, you have done it unto to Me" (Matthew 25:40). Look for opportunities to unveil and release His glory to others in your lives, especially the household of faith.

Each day for you is a new opportunity to train yourself to listen and follow the voice of the Holy Spirit. To capture this same thought, take a look at Romans 8:14, "For as many as are led by the Spirit of God, these are sons of God." You should value these words which are not the words of man, but in truth, they are the words of God. They are living words, supernatural words. It is His words which must have permanent residency within us. His words, which come from the Throne of Glory, radically transform us from the inside out. His words activate the Glory that He already deposited within us. Understand this very rich *pearl* from the Holy Spirit: Without Him we can do nothing. With Him nothing is impossible. Let these words resonate in you.

I wrote this master blueprint so that you could simply receive His wisdom on the glory. He wrote this master blueprint so that you can simply release His manifestations of the glory. That activity in both *receiving* and *releasing* is the wisdom by the Holy Spirit, revealing an invisible river flowing in and multiplying as rivers flowing out. One word to track these images is *"Peace"*. It enters in and then multiplies as it is being released which affects the entire realm He has appointed to you.

It will also be helpful to understand that having two natures is common to everyone. We have the spirit nature and the physical nature. Unless Christ is in us, our spirit is dead to all that God would do through us. We deliberately choose to access the new nature, the nature of Christ, the nature of His glory. His nature is *perfect peace*. It is nothing like anything that is in this world. Every day we face things that create ripples on the pond. Those ripples are common to everyone and are any negative condition that we don't want in our lives; however, you can willfully and deliberately choose the nature of His glory, knowing that without Him you can do nothing, but with Him nothing is impossible.

Enroll into this discipline by the Holy Spirit to train your eyes, your ears, and above all, your mouth with His words that you taste and the ability that you have to discern what is being transformed in that invisible, spiritual realm—His glory. Jesus gave you the same glory He received, so that it is not about any performance by you. Simply continue to trust His glory in you to be revealed and released through your spoken words. Be blessed knowing that you are loved and not forgotten. You have hope that will work within you like good yeast. Take up these words from the Holy Spirit as a new recipe from the Heavenly Father's kitchen and everything will come into alignment with His purposes for you.

For I know the thoughts I think toward you, says the Lord, thoughts of peace and not of evil, to give you a future and a hope. (Jeremiah 29:11)

Bless the Lord, O my soul; And all that is within me, bless His holy name! Bless the Lord, O my soul, And forget not all His benefits: Who forgives all your iniquities, Who heals all your diseases, Who redeems your life from destruction, Who crowns you with lovingkindness and tender mercies, Who satisfies your mouth with good things, so that your youth is renewed like the eagle's. (Psalm 103:1-5 NKJV)

The knowledge of the glory not only benefits you, the individual, but also all those to whom you declare these *pearls* and receive the wisdom, revelation, and knowledge which are given to them by the Father of glory. (Remembering that Jesus has said not to cast your *pearls* before swine for they will just trample on them.) The leading by the Holy Spirit will be detected, as to when and what to say, in any given moment. His leading must overflow from our lives in this way throughout the whole world to be effectively in agreement with the Father's heart, which then manifests His power to transform the conditions. He matches our desire to please Him, much more than we can hope to imagine.

13

Our Relationship Glorifies Jesus

I have a very good friend, John, whom I met while in the US Navy. He was a hospital corpsman and met his future wife who was also in the US Navy. I knew John well enough that I knew his heart and devotion to Jesus. He had been a mentor to me for following the voice of the Holy Spirit. I had mentioned in an earlier chapter that Ron and I had spent time in prayer and fasting before we were sent to go to Massachusetts. (Ron grew up in that area, and had not been back there since he received Jesus.) John was one of them who directed this time of prayer. While I was in Massachusetts, a destination ordained by the Holy Spirit, John had also written me several times.

In one of the letters I received, John had written something that I have never forgotten. He wrote that he had met a navy nurse there in the area where he was stationed. He had assured me that this relationship was of the Lord. These words were what he had written,

"Our relationship glorifies Jesus!" These words should resonate within every one of us. That should be the expression of the Father's Love in us, as it is being mentored in every area of our lives.

In recent years, I have often pondered over those words, and I have discovered that is how He directs us in prayer. We should always speak words that impart into the lives of others. We pray supplicating prayers that should supply the needs of all the saints. This higher ground should be the norm in our walk with the Holy Spirit, making intercession, and prayers of supplication—supplying spirit, soul, and body. "Praying always with all prayer and supplication in the Spirit, being watchful to this end with all perseverance and supplication for all the saints—and for me, that utterance may be given to me, that I may open my mouth boldly to make known the mystery of the gospel" (Ephesians 6:18, 19 NKJV).

Our walk in the Spirit reveals the evidence of the Holy Spirit's work from the testimony that has stood the test of time. We should be more in love with Jesus today than when we first believed. Now He has revealed to us more about His nature, so that you are greatly moved with compassion, knowing that as much as He loves us, it is in spite of how treacherous and deceitful our old natures are. He transforms the mind to walk in the newness of the new man. Without the revelations from the Holy Spirit we would never know the capacity of how great His love is. He chose us and we choose Him. We choose Him above everything else that we could possibly imagine. His love tempers our responses to

Him, in spite of the transitory conditions. "I in them, and You in Me; that they may be made perfect in one, and that the world may know that You have sent Me, and have loved them as You have loved Me" (John 17:23 NKJV). The glory we have is being perfected in our understanding. While following the voice of the Holy Spirit, we can truly say about everything we say and do, "Our relationship glorifies Jesus!"

What we impart in ministry to others is a change of ownership, from us to them. We own it still, but now it has exchanged ownership. They own it now as well. It may make more sense by using this example; Jesus gave His recipe to me, now I own it. It is mine! When I give the same recipe to anyone else, they also own it. It is theirs now! The attitude that He described in possessing a thing is by aggressively and assertively taking it. "The kingdom of heaven is like yeast that a woman **took** and mixed into about sixty pounds of flour until it worked all through the dough" (Matthew 13:33 NIV).

The Father of glory sent His gospel—the gospel of the glory. He entrusted us with this gospel so that it would be imparted to others. The uniqueness of His glory is that it permeates all of our thoughts when it has been activated within us. It consumes us! His glory is manifested in such a way that it is multiplying and spreading like yeast through words that we received from the Holy Spirit, then we speak those inspired words to others who hear and receive this good news of His glory. This brings glory to the Father. Does your relationship glorify Jesus?

The idea behind Jesus' words, "I will make you fishers of men," was to take them to higher ground. He was going to take them into that dimension of His glory, which they had never experienced before. They had been fishermen by trade all their lives, now they were going to enter that supernatural realm to a higher calling more than what they could imagine. They were going to start catching things supernaturally. "...Follow Me, and I will make you become fishers of men" (Mark 1:17 NKJV). Taking what were once common ways of doing things and now bringing them up higher to operate in the Way, and the Truth concerning His glory, so that His Life which is so permeated with theirs caused them to say, "I no longer live, but Christ lives in me."

We may track this theme, *catching things supernaturally*, first of all from the statement, "I will make you fishers of men." Something very insightful is found when Jesus was praying in the garden prior to being arrested—all the disciples were asleep. Mark 14:33 gives us three of the names of those who were asleep: Peter, James, and John. After the third time that Jesus found them asleep, is when the entourage that arrested Him showed up in the garden.

The insight is that John wrote down everything Jesus had prayed while in the garden, but he could not have heard one word of that prayer, for he was asleep during it. This anomaly expresses the truth that John really did *catch things supernaturally*, for all that he wrote in the seventeenth chapter of John came to him by revelation from the Holy Spirit.

We begin utilizing our new found skills in Him to catch things supernaturally, by His glory. We have been working for wages while having holes in our wallets and purses. Now He is going to show us how to work for wages that are ever-increasing, without holes in our wallets and purses. We have been feeding on food that perishes, but He is going to show us how to feed on food that never perishes. "Jesus answered them and said, 'Most assuredly, I say to you, you seek Me, not because you saw the signs, but because you ate of the loaves and were filled. Do not labor for the food which perishes, but for the food which endures to everlasting life, which the Son of Man will give you, because God the Father has set His seal on Him'" (John 6:26, 27 NKJV).

This is not spiritual language with no substance; it is not a form of godliness that denies the power. "For the kingdom of God is not in word but in power" (1 Corinthians 4:20 NKJV). The language is so precise that we miss how accurately Jesus taught His disciples on how to operate in the same glory in which He had been operating. He could do nothing apart from the Father. Everything that the Father does is eternal. It is superlative in every way. Those are the kind of words that are in Jesus' mouth. He told us to put those same words in our mouths, which becomes the stream for the glory to flow and to be directed in and around us.

For the whole creation to be set into a state of futility and chaos, grieves the Father. Yet He has great joy knowing that this heavenly treasure, which cost the greatest amount of any ransom that had ever been paid, is fully, willingly, and efficaciously satisfying forever the schism that breached the heavens into chaos. We are one with the Father and with the very essence of all that He is—the Glory.

The blood is what flowed from His veins; the glory is what flows from ours. This is the exchange that took place in redeeming us. Jesus is fully saturated with the glory of the Father, but He is every bit as human as you and I. When the blood and the glory became one, we gained access to the Father which is available now through the blood that was shed on our behalf. The truth that Jesus declares (remembering that His words are supernatural words), transforms our nature by taking communion with Him. His food is supernatural indeed, and His drink is supernatural indeed. Now we abide in Him, and He abides in us. We are one! The glory is manifested in simplicity through us in the same way that it does through Him. Jesus declared to us that we are to speak His words. When we obey this command, it sets in motion in the supernatural realm all that He told about His disciples—I will make you fishers of men. We are now to operate by catching things in the spirit and not by natural means ever again!

14

Can These Dry Bones Live?

*Y*ou are empowered already; now walk in that kingly-priestly authority. You can now decree and declare. You declare the end from the beginning. You are learning by the Holy Spirit's tutelage to see things in the spiritual realm as completed already. This is the reality that already exists in the heavenly realm. Jesus declared that the kingdom of heaven was within you. It is this glory that the Father deposited in you that operates in the kingdom. Now, you are being thoroughly trained for higher purposes, for noble purposes, for purposes that transform nations. That is the exact language of Jesus, "...make disciples of all the nations" (Matthew 28:19). Engage His glory and deliberately provoke the spiritual realm, knowing He has called you for such a time as this. You are called to impart and awake His glory by speaking words of life over those to whom He sends you.

And He said to me, "Son of man, can these bones live?" So I answered, "O Lord God, You know." Again He said to me, "Prophesy to these bones, and say to them, 'O dry bones, hear the word of the Lord! Thus says the Lord God to these bones: "Surely I will cause breath to enter into you, and you shall live. I will put sinews on you and bring flesh upon you, cover you with skin and put breath in you; and you shall live. Then you shall know that I am the Lord." (Ezekiel 37:3-6 NKJV)

He gave the prophet a *pop quiz* at the end of the class, by saying, "Is there any life in these dry bones?" The answer to this question comes up from the spirit and then aligns with Him. His glory and our words combine which causes us to see any circumstance set before us as His design. Since He orders the steps of the righteous, everywhere that we walk we are given instant opportunity to utilize the wisdom and the knowledge of the glory. It may even be outside our frame of reference and experiences. (Most of the time He does stretch our imaginations), but we know Him. We know His heart and mind. We know that His glory in us transforms every condition. We only need to trust what the Holy Spirit has revealed to us.

The extent of the power of His glory is revealed on purpose to overcome any situation, even if that situation were dead. Jesus was raised from the dead. This should bring the revelation up higher to show us what His glory will do. When we receive this revelation, we are aware that we are totally dependent on Him and His glory. We are learning to perfect and fine-tune all that the Holy Spirit declares to us, so that we can act on His behalf in the circumstances He brings across our paths, whatever they may be.

Everything that entangles the mind and prevents the ability to correspond and commune with His thoughts needs to be set aside, so that His glory rules in the depths of our being. The Holy Spirit is always searching the depths of the Father's heart to convey these truths over to our spirits. Challenge your own eyes and ears by looking into the mirror and declaring the words the Holy Spirit has activated within you. The words should rise up out of your mouth with such force that you know that you know it is the Father's will and His glory in your words.

We are being transformed from glory to glory as we look into the mirror and see the reality of the glory operating in Jesus. We have confidence that this is exactly how His glory works through us. The Father orders the steps of the righteous! He ordered with simplistic detail every step that Jesus walked. Jesus was so aware of this leading that He declared, *I only do what I see the Father doing. I only say what I hear the Father speaking.*

All of this is the language of the glory; it is the Glory speaking to us precisely what the glory is doing in and through us. It is the same way in you! Jesus said, "I am the Way, the Truth, and the Life. No one comes to the Father except through Me" (John 14:6). Fuel is added to Jesus statement, igniting a deeper revelation, when we know that Jesus is the *Lord of glory.* It could be said that, "Jesus is *the Way* the Glory operates, Jesus is *the Truth* concerning the Glory, Jesus is *the Life* of the Glory!"

We know what the Word declares about the nature of God by this one truth: God is Light (1 John 1:5). Knowing that God is Light and that He is also *one* with all of His qualities, we could superimpose this truth onto John 1:1 for our own reflection as follows. "In the beginning was Light, and the Light was with God, and the Light was God . . . and the Light became flesh!" The word *light* is the link to the glory which is in us by the very Scripture found in John 1:4, "In Him was life, and the life was the light of men." That light of men is the glory of the Father.

His glory is hidden, but is intricately woven into the very fabric of His Word from the first page to the last; it is mysteriously being revealed now by every word that the Holy Spirit makes known to us. Additionally, we can link His Word to what was in the Father's mind when He had used three different words to identify with the single-most important event in all of history—the resurrection of Christ, such as Holy Spirit, power, and glory. And again, looking at the foundation, the Word, we can see how the Father thinks, "In the beginning was the Glory, and the Glory was with God, and the Glory was God . . . and the Glory became flesh!"

Now the Glory is in your flesh. You are abiding in Him, and He is abiding in you. You are one with the Father, and the Son. You have the Son; therefore, you have the Father also. We have the Father's glory in us. It is this glory that was manifested. The substance of all of heaven, all that there is, came from the glory being manifested. It was released from the Father when He spoke, "Light be". That same accuracy in flowing with Him is deliberately manifesting His glory and all that is the character and nature of Jesus. We are fused as one! He has made a new creation by taking our personalities, His mind, the Holy Spirit, the glory of the Father, the love of the Father, and sealing us in Him for redemption. It is forever sealed. We are awakened to that image to which He has conformed us. It began when we received Christ, but our place *in Christ*, ignited that new creation.

"And this is eternal life, that they may know You, the only true God, and Jesus Christ whom You have sent" (John 17:3 NKJV). This *knowing* Him is a very intimate knowing. The same language was used when Mary asked, "How can this be seeing I have *known* no man?" He knows our every thought, emotion, and cell of our being. As the Scripture states, "For we are members of His body, of His flesh and of His bones" (Ephesians 5:30 NKJV).

The Holy Spirit is revealing all the nature of the Father through revealing the knowledge of His glory. That knowledge is this very intimate knowledge, knowing Him as we are known. This is our relationship with Him in His glory. We know precisely how His glory operates, and we are given opportunities to experience this through the very Word the Holy Spirit unveils to our spirit. "Beloved, now we are children of God; and it has not yet been revealed what we shall be, but we know that when He is revealed, we shall be like Him, for we shall see Him as He is. And everyone who has this hope in Him purifies himself, just as He is pure" (1 John 3:2, 3 NKJV).

That is why it is very important to connect with what the Father is thinking as recorded in 1 John 3:2. Notice how the phrasing is present tense, "...when He is revealed" and "...as He is". The knowledge we receive is revealed to us in present tense, in the *now*. The hope that, "we shall be like Him", is substantially settled within this same letter in the next chapter, "Love has been perfected among us in this: that we may have boldness in the day of judgment; because as He is, so are we in this world" (1 John 4:17 NKJV).

We know we will be like Him, and we know when this takes place from what the Holy Spirit had revealed to John. Each promise from the Father becomes our basis of experiencing the divine nature—His glory. All that we will ever experience has its foundation through these precious promises. The words that Jesus spoke in prayer are of this same intimate desire for us—that we would come up to where He is—the Throne of Glory, and behold His glory.

15

How Much Are You Believing For?

That word *behold*, in English, doesn't fully express the depth that is in the Father's heart. It is the Greek word, *theóreó*, and has the same root word where we get, *theater;* however, in the context of John 17:22 as we begin to understand that Jesus gave us the glory to make us one with Him and the Father, we also experience the glory on the same stage in which He did. "Father, I desire that they also whom You gave Me may be with Me where I am, that they may *behold* My glory which You have given Me; for You loved Me before the foundation of the world" (John 17:24 NKJV). We are not watching a *fireworks* display that Jesus is presenting, but greater than this, we are intimately *experiencing* all that He has desired for us to have with Him from the beginning of time. We are partaking of the glory; we are one with Him! "To him who overcomes I will grant to sit with Me on My throne, as I also overcame and sat down with My Father on His throne" (Revelation 3:21 NKJV).

Jesus overcame every kind of test as the Lord of glory. Every suffering we are exposed to, He comes to our need immediately. He overcame before and still overcomes now. We are one with Him. We are learning to surrender to this simple place where His glory absolutely overcomes every single realm in which we have been exposed to suffering, even to the slightest degree, but we are not yet acquainted with this level of overcoming in our life experiences. Our minds have not yet understood that it is possible to overcome any challenge set before us. The Holy Spirit imparts the wisdom to us in order to create the steadfast strength and the desires in us from any one single promise that He unveils. Any promise that becomes known to us gives us direct access to enjoy and partake of the divine nature—His glory. It is a living reality to enjoy and partake of His glory just as simply as it is to enjoy and partake of communion.

To understand the Father's heart and thoughts clearly, it is necessary to understand the authority that He has empowered the church with by depositing the glory within us. "To the intent that now the manifold wisdom of God might be made known by the church to the principalities and powers in the heavenly places" (Ephesians 3:10 NKJV). We should be fully aware of how to operate with Him from the Throne of Glory. The purpose for understanding this knowledge of the glory is so that we can take our place as true sons of God.

Let me illustrate the level of authority that is unique when operating in this heavenly realm from the Throne of Glory. Imagine, if you will, that you were the CEO over all the

Walmart stores worldwide. That whole operation, as big as it is, and all the people who work anywhere under the umbrella of your authority would be subject to the kinds of decisions you could make from that authoritative position; however, in my illustration, you cannot walk across the street and exercise that same authority over all the Target employees.

From His Throne of Glory, because there is no other authority that comes in as high, we have total privilege to exercise the authority He has always intended. This privilege would be missed without this knowledge of the glory; We would be no different than slaves as it says in Galatians 4:1. If you really want to see change, then for real, all those who have called on the name of Jesus need to pray and pursue what the Holy Spirit is saying concerning this good news of His glory. Amen! Even if there is understanding in this area, there still needs to be true discipling in training others on how to work with the Holy Spirit in this heavenly realm—His glory. Be blessed in all you say and do. As far as it depends on us, we need to make this our number one priority—yielding to the voice of the Holy Spirit.

Years ago, when I was first married, we had Bible studies in our home each week. On one occasion, the Holy Spirit gave me a word that was related directly to us, but also He revealed later that it was for anyone, in any place, and under any condition. He said, **"If you are bold enough to confess it, then He is big enough to cause it to come to pass."**

That is similar to, "Then the Lord said to me, 'You have seen well, for I am ready to perform My word'" (Jeremiah 1:12 NKJV). In the ESV translation it reads this way, "...You have seen well, for I am watching over my word to perform it."

We had a telecommunications business during that time and always just believed God for success each week, but at first we didn't ask for any specific amount. We were also taking a marriage precept class one day a week. In one of those classes a topic had arisen which captivated our interest—the power of agreement. I believe it is a skill that is useful to any believer, now more than ever, in learning how to be in agreement with the Holy Spirit.

The very next week, I had decided to put this to practice in our business. I asked my wife, Lori, "How many accounts do you believe for this week?"

She replied, "Five." (I actually had a different figure in mind, but I was in agreement.)

I prayed, "Father, we are asking and expecting five accounts this week. Go ministering angels and cause the accounts to come in; satan take your hands off our accounts, they are ours in Jesus' name!"

We went out to do sales and marketing as we had done many times before. The few accounts with whom we had been working for a while had decided to do business with us, so we already had appointments scheduled in advance. At the beginning of the week, we quickly signed up five new accounts, which had appointments on Wednesday that we would still be keeping. It had seemed so effortless doing business this way, with the ease at how we picked up all five accounts, even before the additional appointments; however, when we went to the appointments, every one of the companies had changed their minds about doing business with us for one reason or another.

That night we were at our hotel, I asked the Holy Spirit, "Why were we unable to get any of those accounts with whom we had previous commitments?" He told me, "We had agreed on five, and five is what we had received." I told Lori what the Holy Spirit had said to me, then we prayed again to believe for more; only this time, we did not say any specific amount. The next day, we went out again picking up more accounts to finish up our sales week. I had reflected on the ease we now had with sales compared to the struggle of it in the past. This power of agreement, and learning how to get into agreement through prayer made it exciting to see how it had manifested through what we prayed and declared together.

Preparing for the next week I asked Lori again, "How many accounts are you believing for this week?" This time her reply was fifteen, which had been the same number I had in mind the previous week. We came into agreement, and I prayed in the same manner as I had before, except now I declared that we would have fifteen accounts.

This time, all week long when we went out to do sales, we seemed to struggle getting any signed contracts. So on

Friday morning I talked to the Lord about it, reminding Him that we had prayed and were in agreement for 15 accounts (we only had six accounts, and we were leaving the area at noon, it was 9am.) I said, "I know we have prayed already, but I still expect 15 accounts like we had agreed on and prayed about." Our Father deliberately catches our faith so that we stand in spite of any condition. Ten minutes later, an idea rose up inside me where we might go for sales. We acted on that idea, and before noon, we had exactly fifteen accounts. He is faithful even when we may falter.

The third week practicing this skill—the power of agreement, I asked again, "How many accounts are you believing for this week?" Lori emphatically declares, "Fifteen!" (In my heart I was thinking she was just reacting with her emotions from the exact way the Lord answered our prayers for those 15 accounts from the previous week.) Nevertheless, I chose to be in agreement in spite of how I felt about things. Agreement really is key to operating in any of His promises. I prayed and declared again, "Father, I thank you that we can come together in the power of agreement. We are asking and expecting 15 accounts this week. Go ministering angels, cause the accounts to come in; satan, take your hands off these accounts, they are ours in Jesus' name!"

This was an area that was stretching our faith, because we had never had more than thirteen accounts in any one week in all the previous years we had done business. So to imagine that in back-to-back weeks we would achieve fifteen accounts was unheard of from our experience. God continued to be faithful. The exact amount we declared by the power of agreement is what we received.

You would think that after three weeks in a row, we would be stepping into that new found faith that He was developing in us—the power of agreement, but we never did approach this in doing sales and marketing again until it was winter time. I was pondering over that word I had received from the Holy Spirit in the Bible study, "If you are bold enough to confess it, then He is big enough to cause it to come to pass." This time I remembered and declared what else the Holy Spirit had revealed, about that word being for anyone, any place, and any time no matter what the conditions.

I was willing to put that word from the Holy Spirit to the test by being bold enough to confess it. I asked Lori again, "How many accounts are you believing for this week?" She said nothing, but it is still possible to be in agreement when someone says nothing. I said, "Alright, I am going to believe for 20 accounts this week." I prayed as before and expected exactly what I said to come to pass, even though it was in the middle of winter, the slowest season in our industry. It is astounding to consider that when our Father wants to prove things to us, He does much more than we could ever ask, think, or even imagine. In one day, we had gotten twenty-six accounts. I was amazed! He proves His word, so that we learn to trust Him. We learn to lean on His word and enjoy all the experiences He has always desired for us.

Riches of Glory

16

The Least of These

*J*esus destroyed the works of the enemy, making them useless (come to nothing), but we must enforce this by simply using the name of Jesus. His *Name* is filled and activated with the fullness of the Father's glory. Knowing about His name directly correlates with knowing clearly about His glory. The same authority is manifested through us by His name. Whether by His name or by His word, it is still the glory that is being manifested. We are the ones who are bringing these rulers of darkness to nothing. Each time they manifest, we arrest their work immediately. We are dislodging their habitation, and setting at large the Father's glory to bring the same liberties and freedom that we are presently experiencing into the world around us.

Our walk is one of power and demonstration of the Holy Spirit; it is not filled with empty philosophies that keep people bound, but rather, it is acutely acquainted with these genuinely intimate experiences in Jesus. The whole world is anxiously waiting to experience what we as believers have. Truly, this understanding of the knowledge of the glory is not actively on the mind of most people in the world, but by us having true discernment, we can detect that this is the cry of their heart. Our walk coupled with the manifestations of the Father's glory is what they long to see, because it is the true message of hope that Jesus taught. Not a hope deferred that makes the heart sick, but a living hope that is realized as suffering ends and they stand in victory as the Father's glory is revealed in their lives.

These realities are profound and are being birthed within our spirit by the Holy Spirit. The Spirit searches the deep things of God (1 Corinthians 2:10). Spirit to spirit language is where revelation first takes place, as Scripture says, "Beloved, now we are children of God; and it has not yet been revealed what we shall be, but we know that when He is revealed, we shall be like Him, for we shall see Him as He is. And everyone who has this hope in Him purifies himself, just as He is pure" (1 John 3:2, 3 NKJV). "Love has been perfected among us in this: that we may have boldness in the day of judgment; because as He is, so are we in this world" (1 John 4:17 NKJV). What is revealed concerning Jesus comes from what the Holy Spirit is revealing to us now in this world.

When He reveals to us that we are healed, that revelation begins working its way through us until we are transformed and healed. We see ourselves the way we see Jesus, and are being transformed from glory to glory. This is what purifies the one who was sick. If we saw Jesus as *sickly,* then that revelation would work its way through us; yet, we know the truth about Jesus by the Spirit of Truth, so we know that Jesus was never sick, broke, or lacking any good thing. What we see is what gets manifested in us. And what gets manifested in us, is now on our plate to give to others.

The way Jesus saw what the Father was doing is through this same spirit-to-spirit communication in our lives. The root of this communication has its foundation in the Word, but it's being revealed by the Holy Spirit. It's these *pearls* that become more readily known and understood through discerning His character more accurately. When we experience His wisdom and love through the things that we have suffered, it perfects us.

He does not send the suffering. He sent His Holy Spirit. The Holy Spirit is the one who gives us rich insight to understand the Father's wisdom so that we can intimately experience His glory, which is far greater than any suffering. That is His love language, to intimately experience His glory, to reveal that it is His glory which surrounds us and brings us through any condition as a victor, defeating and destroying the suffering forever. Once that truth is activated within us, we are then able to impart it to others.

Where there is suffering there is more glory. No one wants to suffer, but the focus for Christ was a higher purpose, "who for the joy set before Him endured the cross". That joy, like the same joy in us, is the activated state of His glory, which must be awakened. That is our purpose now among all of our brothers and sisters—to wake up His glory.

This is what He has called us to, for the obtaining of the glory of our Lord Jesus Christ and to restore His glory wherever we are sent. Connect with those of like-minded faith to do what one cannot do alone. One will put to flight a thousand, but the logarithmic proportions is also expressed from glory to glory, in the church and in Christ to all generations forever and ever.

Nothing comes into your realm except as a proving ground for you to be personally trained and developed by the Holy Spirit's wisdom to operate in His glory, so that you know that nothing is impossible. He starts you out on the exact turf in which you are found, for each of us has walked different paths. His very private training has been designed specifically for you. That is why being established in Him has different dimensions; otherwise He would just need to clone us, so that we are like Him. That is not the way of love, for each of us are a unique expression of His love and manifestation of His glory.

I had never written anything before except for classwork years ago. Now not only are there books published, but I also have this strong desire to continue writing more as He continues to reveal more and more. There was a time, though, before I finished writing the first book when I told the Father directly, "Get someone else to write this." It felt overwhelming because I had so many other things going on; I did not imagine I would ever finish, but in my heart I could never truly release what He had placed inside of me. He had already appointed me to write a book. The Father is the one who had motivated me to write it from the very beginning. All the words that I wrote just seemed to flow out of me. This is how receiving wisdom on His glory had been affecting me personally. I had observed that when others began receiving wisdom on His glory, I could mark it on the calendar: in two weeks their lives would never be the same again. This glory wisdom captures our thoughts so much that everything begins to quickly unveil for the first time concerning His glory.

Jesus also received this very private training, "Then Jesus said to them, 'When you lift up the Son of Man, then you will know that I am He, and that I do nothing of Myself; but as My Father taught Me, I speak these things'" (John 8:28 NKJV). The Father taught Jesus, in the same way the Holy Spirit teaches us.

Most preaching and teaching is only done on levels that are *line upon line* and *precept upon precept* as though there was something genuinely profound in what is said. By contrast, nothing is turned into life until faith begins to access the very life of those promises found in Scripture. "For the kingdom of God is not a matter of talk but of power" (1 Corinthians 4:20 NIV).

There is a language that comes alive within us by very practical means when this wisdom and the knowledge of the glory are expressed from the Father's perspective. What has been written means nothing without the Holy Spirit revealing to us; otherwise, it would be just stories and a system of codes and types. Jesus had to open the Scriptures on that road to Emmaus to unveil what was always true about Himself. This truth goes unnoticed; it is just below the current, so that even when we read, it is still missed until He reveals to our spirits.

He is still speaking into existence, but He has sovereignly chosen to speak through the church. Refer to (Ephesians 3:10 and Romans 8:19-22). The orderliness of the kingdom of heaven is always this: *faith, grace,* and *glory.* It is in this order always. The Father's purposes for us, is to manifest His glory. The clear concise language of faith and grace are the means to stand in that place where you may have a hope of His glory being manifested. It is now aligned with the stream of His glory. Make no mistake about it, we are created to manifest His glory in all that we say and do. "Everyone who is called by My name, whom I have created for My glory; I have formed him, yes, I have made him" (Isaiah 43:7 NKJV).

You were created for His glory because you are called by His name. Only those who are called by His name have this royal privilege and high honor which He chose to give to all who are His. "He raises the poor from the dust and lifts the beggar from the ash heap, to set them among princes and make them inherit the throne of glory. For the pillars of the earth are the Lord's, and He has set the world upon them" (1 Samuel 2:8 NKJV).

Notice that those whom He calls, have been among the least on the earth. He chooses in this way because He is abundantly full of love, rich in mercy, and so that no one is left out of His plan in calling us. We respond to that call from this good news concerning His glory. It is the activation life of the Father in the words that gave us birth. It was effortless on our part. We simply received willingly. The same process is true concerning His glory, we simply receive willingly. The Holy Spirit teaches us how to yield in every detail which we continue to receive willingly. Scripture says if the willingness is there it is acceptable according to what one has, not what one does not have. Willingness, I think, is key to establishing anything that the Lord is doing, especially in what brings people closer together. It opens the door, and His glory seals us as one—one heart, one mind, and one vision. That's what the Lord is creating within us when we take communion.

17

Armor of Light

One thing that is very unique concerning His glory and this knowledge of His glory is that it is self-balancing. What I mean by self-balancing is that anything we try to do in our own strength will not produce anything, but in Christ only do we see results. We will know that our relationship with Him is validated when the fruit of His glory manifests. The focus in the past by many has been only a reaction to whatever was outside of their traditions. For instance, if one had prayed for someone to be healed, but the results were anything except healing, then it was naively assumed that it must not be God's will to heal. In spite of those occurrences, the Heavenly Father, who has been rich in mercy and lovingkindness, has also been long-suffering towards those kinds of declarations. Of special note, I have discovered that there is no one who says, "We don't believe in the glory of God." Father God has kept this knowledge of the glory hidden before time began; therefore, it is impossible for the enemy to confuse anyone who is honestly seeking the glory of the Father.

The ability to do things in our own strength is so limited, and can never truly fix anything. But we never have to fix anything in our own strength. We do everything in the power of *His* Strength. Imagine, if you will, what the garden of Eden was like before the fall. What would have been necessary for Adam and Eve to do? We know exactly what would have happened; their days would have remained as heaven on earth. We know these things from what the Holy Spirit is teaching and revealing, but what is even better than knowing what could have been, is knowing that our revelations are filled with greater glory—the glory of the Father, which Jesus had from the beginning of time. This glory created all that there is. The Holy Spirit is giving private tutoring lessons on how to work with the Father as His glory operates in us, through us, and all around us.

That is why we need to be empowered with the same wisdom, the same authority, the same keen insight that the Holy Spirit knows, in ways that no one could possibly know. We not only taste this wisdom—His glory knowledge, but we also see the results, which have the same supernatural signature that followed Jesus' life. Now this is the signature that follows our lives. The priority for us now is to teach and impart His wisdom and knowledge concerning His glory as it is pre-eminent above everything that we could possibly receive. His glory is above all the heavens and the earth; therefore, this knowledge of the glory is above all that we could possibly know.

I used to water ski quite often every summer with various friends who would ask me how I got the spray so high. My answer to them would be, "If you ski right, the spray is right." The knowledge of the glory, being higher than everything else, puts an alignment in anyone's heart who is truly hungry for God, regardless of what their particular background or understanding from the past has been. So to simplify this, "If you teach right, then the results are right." The Holy Spirit gave me a word some time ago which gave rich insight to seeing those kinds of results well in advance; *"Recognize where they are and rejoice in where Jesus is taking them!"*

There were other times when I had been asked, "How do you ski so well?" where my response was, "I ski to the glory of God!" This would be true. Many times out on the river, before skiing, I would place the handle between my legs and raise my hands, thanking the Father and giving praise to Him.

When my friends asked that question, my answer was the same, "I ski to the glory of God. Isn't that what you do?"

They would reply, "No."

My facetious response to that was, "I can't believe all my skiing friends are heathen. What's the matter with you guys!" I think it is the lightheartedness blended with truth that opens up the door for others to receive what we possess.

Jesus tells us to go and make disciples. Making disciples is not about only getting them saved. He is saying for us to teach them, by all that we have observed through what the Holy Spirit has revealed to us. In His own life, Jesus said,

Either believe the words I say, or believe the works I do. That is what we teach, both the words of the Lord of glory and the works of the Lord of glory that are manifested in our own lives. What we have on our own plate is what we bring to others. If it is not on our plate then it is only theory and lacks the vitality and life-force of the Father of glory Himself.

Without a vision from the Lord people perish, they fail, or they get off in some ditch somewhere. Is this you? We do not want to miss out on what He is doing and imparting to us now. We need this vision burning so brightly inside of us that we will have clarity in everything we say and do. Here is the vision: *"The whole earth will be filled with the knowledge of the glory of the Lord."* To accurately account for this, the whole church does not even have this wisdom, revelation, and knowledge of His glory; therefore, the vision directs us to start waking up the church! Are you with me in this?

If a few believers have this vision so precisely imparted within them, then I truly believe these books that He has had me write will become very effective tools to enhance all that the Holy Spirit is doing to prepare the body of Christ for a great awakening—a complete reformation. No longer will it be only disciples who are added but disciples who have multiplied. Notice the language is not *believers* but *disciples* who have the disciplines of the Holy Spirit's wisdom, nature, and glory to impart to others. He quickly rearranges their lives supernaturally. In truth, everything happened by Him authoring the story of their lives. He did it with these *pearls* from His glory at an accelerated rate. The nature of His glory effortlessly multiplies and transforms us; it completely permeates the total being with an increase that is exactly like those qualities we have come to understand about yeast.

> And do this, knowing the time, that now it is high time to awake out of sleep; for now our salvation is nearer than when we first believed. The night is far spent, the day is at hand. Therefore let us cast off the works of darkness, and let us put on the armor of light. Let us walk properly, as in the day, not in revelry and drunkenness, not in lewdness and lust, not in strife and envy. But put on the Lord Jesus Christ, and make no provision for the flesh, to fulfill its lusts. (Romans 13:11-14 NKJV)

I started the first book in this series which took a little more than three years before I finished in 2012 on Thanksgiving Day. There were times I told the Lord directly, "Get someone else to write this book." I knew it was extremely important and that it was very anointed, so in my heart I could never really release it, even though I had said what I said. After I finished that first book, right away, I began writing the second in the series. Three months later I had completed writing the second book. That by itself was very significant to me. It was not planned that way, it just happened that way. So what took a little more than three years to write the first, the second was done in three months.

The knowledge of the glory is very similar in pattern, like the knowledge of faith, however, it is accelerated. That is why there seems to be a distinct difference in what we see happening in Jesus' life and ours. The same things in our lives do not seem to have immediate results as it did time and time again in Jesus' life. Glory knowledge is different; it is this knowledge of the glory that will be known throughout the whole earth. The more we hear and perceive all that the Holy Spirit is revealing to us, the more we understand how to work with Him in the Glory. Jesus said it this way—He could do nothing apart from the Father.

The glory is in the light spectrum by definition, with terms like, *kingdom of light, Light of the world*, and also *Father of lights*. We know that light travels at 186,000 miles per second. It is also known that the farthest reaches of the universe to be measured by scientists is 13.7 billion light years. That is the distance that light travels in 13.7 billion years. His glory is above all the heavens and the earth, which means the Throne of Glory is at least 13.7 billion light years away. Jesus ascended to heaven to be with the Father. If He were traveling at the speed of light that would be 6 times around the earth in one second, or the same speed the internet transports information, such as an email. If you were to send an email to the Father of glory it would take 13.7 billion years just to reach Him and that is if He answered immediately. In the glory realm, this all points to one thing, there is something about the acceleration in His glory that we do not as yet understand. His glory comes in higher, faster, and more powerful than anything we could hope to imagine. Yet the Father Himself has given us direct access to this kingdom of light and has qualified us, so that at any time we can come boldly before His throne. We are seated with Christ on the throne now. All answers to prayer are accelerated because of His glory; therefore, the more we know about His glory, the greater application with deeper adoration we will experience in our daily lives.

That is why Jesus has engaged our own walk right from the beginning, by giving us the same glory. "And the glory which You gave Me I have given them, that they may be one just as We are one" (John 17:22 NKJV). This is also stated in Matthew but missed, because the knowledge of the glory is what unveils this truth. "And Jesus came and spoke to them, saying, 'All authority has been given to Me in heaven and on earth'" (Matthew 28:18 NKJV). What He received has been given to us. It is the work of the Holy Spirit to declare to us within our spirit-man the words of the Father so that it becomes activated in our lives.

Jesus said that we would be perfected in His glory and perfected in how we work with Him. That condition is set in motion, knowing that the Father loves us in the same way He loves Jesus. This wisdom is what perfects us. It will take us through any condition set before us. "I in them, and You in Me; that they may be made perfect in one, and that the world may know that You have sent Me, and have loved them as You have loved Me" (John 17:23 NKJV). He was perfected in the things He suffered, to the point that He had complete joy in going to the cross. We have the same joy and carry our own cross. Our training is very personal, very intimate from the Holy Spirit. Every word from Him is life that is imparted, and transforms our whole being, though it is designed for us individually. I carry my own cross knowing in advance that His glory is greater.

Riches of Glory

18

Hitchhiker's Guide to the Glory

*C*ross-pollination is developed through us as a promotion, such as *receive a prophet in the name of a prophet, and receive that prophet's reward.* The kingdom has increased and accelerated by love. When we genuinely receive that prophet, then what is on that prophet's plate, now manifests on ours. It is like a spice that has been added to our recipe!

Here is an extremely valuable truth, which separates from everything else that seemingly sounds spiritual out there. Many will say that God is in all of us, whether or not, we can declare a much higher truth. Not only is Christ in us, the hope of glory, but also we are in Christ. That last part, *We are in Christ* is true to every believer who has been awakened. His glory is no longer lying dormant in us—inactive. It is no longer a hope. It is no longer an imperishable seed in seed form. It is no longer this treasure *in* earthen vessels. The *in Christ* experience AWAKENED from the words that the Holy Spirit spoke, and it rose up out of us. First it was in our heart, now it is radiating out of our mouths. "Looking unto Jesus, the author and finisher of our faith, who for the joy that was set before Him endured the cross, despising the shame, and has sat down at the right hand of the throne of God" (Hebrews 12:2 NKJV).

For it was fitting for Him, for whom are all things and by whom are all things, in bringing many sons to glory, to make the captain of their salvation perfect through sufferings. (Hebrews 2:10 NKJV)

Then He said to them all, "If anyone desires to come after Me, let him deny himself, and take up his cross daily, and follow Me. For whoever desires to save his life will lose it, but whoever loses his life for My sake will save it. (Luke 9:23, 24 NKJV)

The glory is the very substance He had deposited within us which is more than words. His glory is there to be activated in every circumstance. He has *wired* His glory to coincide with our spoken words. This is why Jesus said, "If you abide in Me, and My words abide in you, you will ask (and declare) whatever you will, and it will be done for you." Then He said (with words that come directly from the Father) "I have told you these things so that My joy may be in you, and that your joy may be full." The joy is a result of that manifestation from the Father, either by words or by works, for both have that same life.

I was with two friends, Dave and Randy, one evening. We had been out to a restaurant earlier, enjoying the fellowship and the Word. When we decided to leave it was early in the morning. I chose to sit in the back of the vehicle (having been up long hours, two days in a row). I was exhausted and just wanted to rest. As we were headed down the highway, my friend, Randy, pulls over to pick up a hitchhiker.

Dave and this new passenger became engaged in deep conversation about God. At some point, Randy decided to stop the car; all three of them got out of the vehicle and continued talking about the things of God. We were parked in a turn around, and I stayed in the vehicle, semi-awake. I could faintly hear their conversations in the background. Suddenly, their conversation had turned to being more specifically about Jesus rather than just about God. The nature of this hitchhiker changed from one that was cerebral to one that was vehemently filled with rage. He had become so hostile, I was surprised the conversation continued. It was upon hearing the name of Jesus that caused the sudden change in the hitchhiker's temperament. The rage that had manifested through this individual they had picked up alongside the road was a reaction to the powerful name of Jesus.

What had been an exhausted, half awakened, catatonic state with me was now complete alertness; I was wide awake! I had a witness in my spirit that this man was demon-possessed, and knew exactly what I would do (Before this occasion, I had hoped that I would never meet up with anyone who was demon-possessed.) I got out of the vehicle and walked directly to where Dave, Randy, and this other man were standing. The hitchhiker was an enormous black man both in size and height, so he towered over me. He was still extremely hostile in his voice and demeanor. Looking up at him, I simply said, "Let me ask you this, has Jesus Christ come in the flesh?"

Instantly, he went from this enraged hostile personality to one that was completely docile, almost like a whipped puppy. I asked him again, "Has Jesus Christ come in the flesh?" He wouldn't answer me, so my next thought was to cast the devil out of him, but what I said was, "In the name of Jesus, I command you to go!" And he walked away. I was dumbfounded! I was unsure why that had happened. (I know now what to expect, and that our words have tremendous authority in the spiritual realm because of Jesus. Words are extremely accurate too.)

We were close enough to where our pastor lived, and we surmised it was still early enough that he might be awake. We knew he had dealt with demons in his own walk with the Lord. He would be able to give us more insight as to what we had experienced, so we drove over to his place and knocked on the door. He was already up.

When these demons manifest, we have authority over them, but they will try to deceive us so that we don't have authority; however, just mentioning the Blood or the name of Jesus makes them cringe. He graces our lives exactly when we need it. Until this experience, it had been very unsettling for me to think of dealing with demonic spirits. "And of His fullness we have all received, and grace for grace" (John 1:16 NKJV).

That experience settled the truth forever in my spirit that I do have authority over these demons, and the way that it felt was not unlike how I would speak to a stray dog that was on my porch, by declaring, "Get out of here!"

The basis for understanding our authority, and the ability to command things in the name of Jesus, has its roots founded in this verse in 2 Corinthians 4:6, "For it is the God who commanded light to shine out of darkness, who has shone in our hearts to give the light of the knowledge of the glory of God in the face of Jesus Christ." The uniqueness of how the Father operates in the spiritual realm is not always caught. When it comes to spiritual matters, the Father who is Spirit, breathes, speaks, and commands.

The Holy Spirit is teaching us accurately all that comes from the Throne of Glory. This revelation should be alive in our experience; we too, command things in His glory. Our experiences do not dictate His glory; His glory dictates our experiences. We are separated out by the Holy Spirit for this special training and guidance in the knowledge of the glory. It could be compared to receiving a four-year scholarship ride from some major college. In this case, we are getting specialized training by the Holy Spirit, working directly with Him in the knowledge of the glory. He has separated us for this exact purpose. "...Ask Me of things to come concerning My sons; and concerning the work of My hands, you command Me" (Isaiah 45:11 NKJV).

He sends us out with those words of reconciliation, words to restore, to begin operating in His glory from the very first word He had spoken to us. It is His wisdom and our words that have become immersed in His glory. Practical application in which anyone can immediately walk, is declaring exactly what you expect, as high as you expect, without wavering in the very words that are spoken.

Learning the language of the glory by commanding things, e.g., "Be healed!", fuses these revelations by the Holy Spirit from one level of glory to the next level of glory. It transforms our thinking and it transforms the conditions. It lifts us up into a greater understanding of things in the spiritual realm. We are not the sick trying to get healed; that kind of thinking falls far short of this language of the glory. God spoke, it became, and He saw that it was good. That is how Jesus operated, and the Holy Spirit is teaching us that we also operate in this way—we speak and things become. We see His goodness manifested by what we say.

God commanded the light; He spoke and light became. In 2 Corinthians 4:6 and Genesis 1:3 the Holy Spirit has revealed to us that the Father *commanded*. I believe the Holy Spirit wants to bring us up higher in this language—to command; He wants to elevate our thinking and experiences so that we utilize our ability to COMMAND.

For example, we would say with command, "Be healed", or "Be blessed". He is not telling us to stop praying or using the name of Jesus. (His word is interwoven so that all truth has become the fabric of who we are.) He is just isolating and identifying the significance of this *command* revelation so that we can step into it with greater authority. This language of His glory is what the Father had spoken. He commanded the light to manifest by saying, "Light be!" There is a greater emphasis when we command. "Ask Me of things to come concerning My sons; and concerning the work of My hands, you command Me" (Isaiah 45:11 NKJV).

Jesus declared the truth of what we have received when His glory was deposited into us. "All things that the Father has are Mine. Therefore I said that He will take of Mine and declare it to you" (John 16:15 NKJV). What originally came from the Father is now being declared to us by the Holy Spirit. The Father commanded the glory to manifest. The Holy Spirit declares this revelation to our spirit because we are in Christ. Now we have received this wisdom and knowledge of the glory, so that we may operate with greater authority in every area of our lives.

Riches of Glory

19

Master Carpenter

W hen I travelled to Korea with a small group of
believers to visit what was at the time the largest
church in the world (at the time of this writing it is
still), we sat in the English-speaking section. We had
headphones on so that we could understand what was
taking place. There were many significant things that stood
out in that service. One thing that greatly impressed me was
how many times prayer took place throughout the service.
The kind of authority that was expressed through prayer
could not be mistaken. The order of that service was
engaging from the very beginning when the very first
declaration was made that commanded people to give their
lives to Jesus. Several hundred people came forward to
receive Christ.

The prophet Ezekiel was commanded by the Lord to
command life into those dry bones. "Again He said to me,
"Prophesy to these bones, and say to them, 'O dry bones,
hear the word of the Lord!' So I prophesied as I was

commanded; and as I prophesied, there was a noise, and suddenly a rattling; and the bones came together, bone to bone" (Ezekiel 37:4, 7 NKJV).

It is this knowledge of the glory that is unique to everything that the Father is doing. He is restoring life where there was no life. The glory raised Jesus from the dead. Before Jesus had been raised from the dead, He revealed His nature, the nature of the glory, when He commanded Lazarus to be raised from the dead. Notice the language from what Jesus commanded in His conversation with Martha, "Did I not say to you that if you would believe you would see the glory of God? Now when He had said these things, He cried with a loud voice, 'Lazarus, come forth!'" (John 11:40,43 NKJV).

We see in this verse that Jesus commanded Lazarus to come forth. Yet the passage also reveals that He had prayed just before giving that command. Every word the Holy Spirit reveals gives greater insight for operating in the knowledge of the glory. The place we should stand prior to commanding anything is the grace of knowing the Father always hears us, and that we have His favor. "...Father, I thank You that You have heard Me. And I know that You always hear Me, but because of the people who are standing by I said this, that they may believe that You sent Me" (John 11:41, 42 NKJV).

It has come to my understanding that we are not only revealing His manifold wisdom to the demonic realm, but more importantly, we are revealing the wisdom, and the knowledge of His glory to God's holy angels. The reality of this is that before He had ever revealed this knowledge of His glory, it was always a mystery. Now He has chosen that His saints would have direct access into understanding all that was Jesus' desire as revealed in His prayer that is recorded in John 17. The glory has been reserved for this New Creation, His saints, the children of light.

"Everyone who is called by My name, whom I have created for My glory; I have formed him, yes, I have made him" (Isaiah 43:7 NKJV). This verse gives three actions God has taken concerning those who are called by His name for glory: He created, formed, and made us. Each of these is a specific area that He has designed as we are being fitted and qualified for His glory. This took place instantly in the *new creation*. The *form* is the image of Christ that is being manifested through us as it is expressed through any condition. Finally, He *made* us through all that the Holy Spirit has unveiled to us. The Holy Spirit gives insight, wisdom, and understanding into all that the Father has already deposited in us—His glory.

Jesus is holy, for the Father is holy. He is not missing any parts; He is complete in His glorified body. Neither are we missing any parts, but we do lack wisdom and knowledge in the spiritual realm, these intimate experiences in Jesus, and it is the ministry of the Holy Spirit to make this known. We are more than qualified and more than conquerors in the spiritual realm. Intimate experiences in Christ prove His glory to us and others. Even if others truly believe in their hearts and believe the truth in their minds, their own intimate experiences validate what they believe. If someone had never tasted my pizza then they have no ability to tell others how good it is, even if they believe it to be. His glory is greater than my pizza. We are blessed that He has chosen to give us the glory of the Father.

> Everyone who is called by My name, whom I have created for My glory; I have formed him, yes, I have made him. (Isaiah 43:7 NKJV)

> And now, O Father, glorify Me together with Yourself, with the glory which I had with You before the world was. . .And the glory which You gave Me I have given them, that they may be one just as We are one. (John 17:5, 22 NKJV)

The kingdom of darkness does not have a clue how to operate in His glory. They only mimic what they see operating in us. There are false signs, wonders, and miracles that manifest in the kingdom of darkness, but we are the ones who deliberately operate in the Truth. There are true signs, wonders, and miracles that are unmistakable, so that the whole world knows that Jesus is alive today, living through us. If any have hardened their hearts, the Father makes this His burden, not ours, but we are to remain faithful to Him regardless.

When the Holy Spirit reveals anything to us, it is perfecting our understanding in His glory. The Bible word for this is called sanctification. He is sanctifying us so that we are useful to Him in every way. We think right and we act right; not by our own inertia to think right or act right, but as an afterglow from His glory streaming through us. We delight in following Him by His Love which establishes who we are. This Love directs and perfects us; it rules in us, instead of our own rules that we come up with in attempt to make boundaries for the old nature. That is of the old nature still trying to measure. God's answer for the old nature is always the same—the old nature must die. He told us clearly to take note how we measure. We are to measure by His peace, joy, and love which activate within our spirits and radiate out of this new creation—the nature of being one with Him.

We have this calling that the Holy Spirit is perfecting by separating us for a higher purpose. Not unlike how someone would be separated to study in college on a four year full ride scholarship. The Holy Spirit is our private tutor for training and leading us into the knowledge of His glory. This kind of training only comes from Him. He has designed everything tailored to suit us perfectly so that it is simple and clear for understanding the knowledge of His glory. It should be simple enough that even second graders would know and understand.

An example of the 2nd grade curriculum, is this, "All have sinned and fall short of the glory of God" (Romans 3:23); however, the Father did not create us to sin, nor to fall short of the glory. Jesus restored the glory, which is the gift He gave us (John 17:22). It is true all have sinned, but it is also true that He created us to enjoy all that He enjoys. The accuracy for the 2nd graders could be followed as this; hold your hands above your head and say, " All have sinned." Now move your hands to your shoulders and say, "Now Christ is my head and I am seated with Him in heavenly places." The *glory line* has been moved. My head is above that *glory line.* Now, I am no longer falling short of His glory. I can see above the glory line. I can see how Jesus sees things.

You should know beyond all your wildest imaginations that Jesus restored the glory. Our new natures are the nature of Christ. We have the same glory He has. Whatever His glory does and did through Him, now does through us. His Word is filled with Glory. His Word and His Glory are ONE. When we speak His word, we are releasing glory. Whatever the Father does, His glory does. His glory does the same through us as His glory does through Him. We are vessels of His glory in the same way Jesus said He could do nothing apart from the Father. The heavenly wiring that accurately empowers us in the same way is this: the Father is in Me and I am in the Father.

In the spirit realm our eyes of faith are more complex than these physical eyes He designed for us. We have the ability to focus directly on Him, on His Glory, and on His righteousness. Our eyes are perfected in those areas where we focus the most. They are one of the main sensory points that bring input from our world around us. "But we all, with unveiled face, beholding as in a mirror the glory of the Lord, are being transformed into the same image from glory to glory, just as by the Spirit of the Lord" (2 Corinthians 3:18 NKJV).

Our physical body is a blueprint for the spiritual body. The blueprint is not the structure; it only tells us how the structure is made. Upon looking more precisely at the blueprint through the eyes of the Master Carpenter, we gain insight and wisdom as to how the spiritual structure is built. For instance, the eyes in our physical body are the blueprint as to how we see things in the spirit. We keep our eyes on His word, which is the truth and accuracy of how things are operating in the spiritual realm. In Romans 5:2, we see this blueprint pattern all throughout Scripture: *faith—grace—glory*. Faith accesses the garage parking lot, grace places us in any suite we desire, and we come up even higher to the executive suites in His glory. "Therefore, having been justified by faith, we have peace with God through our Lord Jesus Christ, through whom also we have access by **faith** into this **grace** in which we stand, and rejoice in hope of the **glory** of God" (Romans 5:1, 2 NKJV).

20

Specialized Curriculum

*T*he pattern formed in Scripture by the Holy Spirit to enter into the joy of the Lord over every single condition is presented in one clear snapshot in Romans 5:2. We access by faith. We stand by grace. We rejoice in the hope of the glory. Rejoicing is evidence that His glory in us has been activated. The only reason it is still hope, is that these two truths must be knitted together in the spirit realm coming up from our hearts as we declare from our mouths, "Without You I can do nothing. With You nothing is impossible." The complete picture in a word—GLORY. While that is true, it is not known; it is elusive and not working through our spirit as though it were the very life of us. He has unfolded His glory so that we can gain spiritual wisdom and insight, and connect in a way that it is no longer elusive, but a reality with intimate experiences that can be imparted to others.

Unfolding that one word GLORY is first looked at under the microscope as *Grace* and *Truth*. "And the Word became flesh and dwelt among us, and we beheld His glory, the glory as of the only begotten of the Father, full of grace and truth" (John 1:14 NKJV). He is the Father of glory, so that everywhere we see "Father," (as related to heavenly Father) in Scripture, we are also talking about Glory. Even when it says Father of lights, or Father of spirits, it is still revealing His Glory. He is Spirit, so when we worship in *Spirit* and *Truth*, we have entered directly into the presence of His Glory. More of His Glory unfolds before us just by knowing He is Father, including grace, truth and spirit. The more you know about these words, the more you know about His glory. By putting the pieces together as they unfold such as *Spirit* and *Truth* through worship, we are receiving direct revelation of His glory and experiencing direct manifestations of His glory by acting on this axiom truth in His kingdom—**Two become ONE**. Any time Two become ONE, Glory is manifested. Here are the Two: *Spirit* and *Truth.* When they become ONE, Glory is manifested.

He is the Father of Lights, but we know we are still talking about the Father of Glory, so when He unveils to us more about Light, we know He is revealing His glory. Jesus is the Perfect revelation and the *exact image* of His Glory. When Jesus speaks, it is the glory speaking. What Jesus does, it is the glory doing something. The very Life of Jesus is the very Life of the glory. If you have invited His Life into your life, you have invited the glory into your life. You have been born-again by imperishable seed. That seed is the seed of His glory to be awakened within, activated by words that come from the Holy Spirit. Only His words awaken the glory within us. His words are glory wisdom that come from the Throne of Glory. Listening to the voice of the Holy Spirit, is listening to a steady stream of glory wisdom and glory works to be manifested through us. This steady stream is rising up from within us, and flows from us in the exact way it flowed from Jesus, such that He says, I only do what I see my Father doing. I only say what I hear my Father saying. When we are *in Christ* we are in His Glory where we can see what the Father is doing and hear what the Father is saying.

Peace is so very real that it creates such a stillness within. Anything that is not that stillness is detected immediately, and we know it is NOT Him. Distractions do not take away our Peace but reveal the truth about conditions set before us. In the spirit realm we can come back to still waters through worship and prayer that transforms an unsettling disturbance, because the whole realm, which had the uneasy, unsettling turmoil became exposed to His glory through us. That exposure to His glory manifests Peace to everyone in that overflow that is coming from us. We have this authority like no one else throughout His entire creation. We are created for glory, and the Spirit of Glory absolutely teaches us how to operate with wisdom in the very authority that Jesus poured out His blood for, to make sure that we would never fall short of the glory ever again. That is how much He loves us, beyond anything that we could ever imagine. Without You I can do nothing! With You nothing is impossible! I love you Father God!

When He declared that He would write His laws on our hearts, I wonder if it is ever considered that the One who is writing is the very One who has *framed* the universe by His spoken word. We have become His house. The framing that

He set up truly was His laws. This could be easily compared to the Master Carpenter using dimension lumber. The finishing work is actually done by the Holy Spirit. We can accurately base this on Jesus' own words, "I still have many things to say to you, but you cannot bear them now. However, when He, the Spirit of truth, has come, He will guide you into all truth; for He will not speak on His own authority, but whatever He hears He will speak; and He will tell you things to come" (John 16:12, 13 NKJV).

If you can follow the Father's work here, you will note that Jesus left the initial work to be completed by the Holy Spirit. We come along working with the Holy Spirit as He guides us, and we are still using the same tools that He used from the beginning—His spoken word. Willfully declare His words as you walk out this wisdom and knowledge of His glory. Jesus said that you would be able to validate the reality of this truth by doing just that: willfully doing His will. In simple terms, it only means we follow the blueprint He laid out before us. Ask yourself, how did He change the water into wine? The answer to this question will set you on course to operating with Him in your very first manifestation of His glory with the knowledge of how to work with Him again and again. You will not only be able to work *with* Him, but also what you receive, you will be able to impart to others.

We have a specialized curriculum specifically created and designed by the Holy Spirit. It is suited individually for each of us to operate in the manifestations of His glory that He has prepared in advance for us, so that we could rejoice in the fullness of Him in us, and impart this to others. The end result: it glorifies the Father—from glory to glory. *Suited individually* in precept is exactly what Scripture says in several places, such as, "but all the members of that one body, being many, are one body" (1 Corinthians 12:12) and again in the same chapter "There are diversity of gifts, but the same Spirit" (1 Corinthians 12:4). Nature gives another example that is easy to capture: there are many snowflakes, but no two are exactly alike. Though all are small, white crystals, the differences are unnoticeable until closely examined. The Holy Spirit is leading you differently than He is leading me or any other believer; however, He is the one Teacher who is teaching everything that comes from the Throne of Glory. The end result is that we learn how to work with Him and how to speak in alignment with Him. Jesus had this same kind of training.

He knows you so intimately, and every step of your life is not like anyone else's. He created you wonderfully, and that uniqueness is revealed through how your spirit, soul, and physical being come into alignment with this knowledge of His glory. No one else in the entire universe is exactly like you. He created you for His glory, and how His glory is being manifested through you is completely unique to you alone. "Everyone who is called by My name, whom I have created for My glory; I have formed him, yes, I have made him" (Isaiah 43:7 NKJV).

The Word that is fused to our souls will overshadow all of our thinking because of the yieldedness already in our spirit. We step out of the way, and the Word fuses to our soul; without any effort on our part we are thinking things that were once impossible, but now they are not. We are believers now, believing the impossible, even if it is against all physics, scientific evidence, doctor's diagnosis, and/or worldly intellectuals. His word supersedes everything else, in spite of the opposition that tries to prove differently. His word is creative life-force within us that changes everything. That is the excellency of the power of His glory. We have these riches within, both the wisdom and the power of His glory, for Christ is in us.

> For Jews request a sign, and Greeks seek after wisdom; but we preach Christ crucified, to the Jews a stumbling block and to the Greeks foolishness, but to those who are called, both Jews and Greeks, Christ the power of God and the wisdom of God. Because the foolishness of God is wiser than men, and the weakness of God is stronger than men. (1 Corinthians 1:22-25 NKJV)

Practice this one word—*yieldedness*. It is the totality of our relationship in Him. We begin to know Him more when we truly know how to yield to Him, and it overflows in how well we yield to one another. Here is an example of yielding to Him: you have made apple pie, and Jesus has come over to your place for a visit. You already know that He does not really like apple pie. This knowledge rearranges your thinking, so you begin to prepare something that you know He does like. You are yielded. Not because you are trying to obey Him, but out of love to serve Him. Your marionberry pie has pleased Him by far, because you chose to delight in making something He does like, instead of thinking you will serve Him apple pie simply because it is already made.

21

Light for my Path

*L*et me state this wisely, when we are His, we are totally yielded. We yield in ways that serve Him, and we serve others. The greatest then is he who truly serves. A person who truly serves is truly yielded. A person who serves only himself is not only unyielded, but he will be the Lord's concern. In our hearts we know it is neither good nor acceptable nor perfect. We have authority to bless and release others, not to dominate others. We have dominion only in the spiritual realm, taking our place with the Father as the Holy Spirit teaches us how to work with Him, His word and His glory. We are manifesting the kinds of glory fruit that totally pleases the Father. We only do what we see the Father of glory doing; we only say what we hear the Father of glory speaking.

Think about this, because your spirit already knows the truth, it rings with truth whenever you hear any truth. Our minds have not filtered these thoughts from the Father yet, so even though our spirit agree with one another, our minds are not yet transformed to think in such a way. It is foreign to our thinking, and it is definitely foreign to the way that we speak. He is streaming His creative words through these vessels of honor, vessels of glory. When His word comes streaming through us, at that moment it begins to transform our thinking.

You do not have to be told that Jesus went to be with the Father. You already know He went to the Father. That is Holy Spirit language that has created the transformation within you. It is revelatory to your nature and transformed you effortlessly. You do not have to try to figure it out. You know that you know—it is truth. Jesus ties that truth together with this truth; the moment you know that Jesus went to the Father, you have direct access to the greater works. This truth is revolutionary in its application, and it is the work of the Holy Spirit who imparted it. Now test out the veracity of the wisdom from the Father by acting on it. Command things in the realm that is subject to the word of glory (the words of Jesus in you) and watch that it obeys you. You have just energized and taught your spirit-man how to be permeated with words of Life. Your mind is renewed from acting on His word which has supernatural results in the natural realm.

It is *not hard to act and think like* Jesus, the Holy Spirit tells us the same things He told Jesus, and we have the same glory Jesus has. We have wisdom from the Holy Spirit on how to work with Him in His glory. The glory of Christ in us does two things simultaneously and effortlessly on our part: it puts to death our old nature, and it ignites our new nature. We have two natures. The Father has made us totally dependent on Him to know the nature of His glory, as well as our old nature. The nature of His glory is exactly like Christ. We never had wisdom before on how to operate with Him in His glory until the Holy Spirit spoke words to renew and realign our thinking with how the Father thinks. This same signature that followed Jesus' life, now follows our lives.

We have no problem that is unique to us individually, but we all have the same old nature. "The heart is deceitful above all things, and desperately wicked; who can know it?" (Jeremiah 17:9 NKJV). Our new nature is the nature of Christ, the nature of the glory. We still have our old nature though which makes it a challenge when trying anything in our own strength. The dying of Christ in us is putting the old nature to death. His death is the only death that will. Even Jesus did not die right away on the cross, and we have the life of Christ within us. This is the new creation life, in which our minds have not yet been renewed in every thought. Through every opportunity to engraft His word, the Holy Spirit is declaring to us, so that our minds are renewed by acting on what He reveals and by manifesting His glory. "Oh, taste and see that the Lord is good; blessed is the man who trusts in Him!" (Psalm 34:8 NKJV).

The Holy Spirit gives us practical application on how to think like the Father thinks. By using our spiritual eyes and ears that have been highly developed through working with the Holy Spirit, we can discern what things are good, acceptable, and perfect. Concerning the things that we see and hear that do not line up with the heart and mind of the Father, the Holy Spirit will ignite His word inside of us to begin transforming our minds. We speak in agreement with Him, and this releases His glory in us. Even if it is the most impossible situation or circumstance, His glory is still greater.

One evening after sunset, another friend and I chose to go over to a Christian couple's home who were mutual friends of ours. We had gone hunting together in the past, and it has always been enjoyable to edify one another in the Word. "As iron sharpens iron, so a man sharpens the countenance of his friend" (Proverbs 27:17 NKJV). Fellowshipping with others who are like-minded will develop and fine-tune how we perceive things in the Spirit.

Their place was on a dimly lit side street. You would have to know the area well enough in order to walk around in the dark and not stumble. When we pulled up in the vehicle and got out, I decided to walk between two vehicles that were already parked there and then make my way across the short footbridge that crossed over the creek. I had been here several times before and knew my way around fairly easily, even though it was almost pitch-black outside. I could barely see the outline of the house. As I started out, I suddenly felt this sensation that went blindly stabbing into my right eye. The pain was excruciating! Somehow, the antenna from one of the cars was angled downward and into the narrow path between the two. It was at just the right height so that the antenna plunged underneath my eyeball and into the back of the eye socket. It was not only the antenna, but also the knob on the end of it that had been pushed to the back of my eye. A piercing brightness like a lightning bolt numbed and temporarily blinded my eye from that extrusion. I groped my way to the door, while my friend guided me to the porch. Our friend's who lived there were of course totally unaware of what had just happened until they opened the door to my agonizing pain and plight.

Cecil and his wife were spiritually mature. They knew how to pray and believe for healing. Upon hearing the news of what took place outside, they laid hands on me and began to boldly pray. The pain left immediately! But there was still a slight wincing irritation when I blinked from the foreign, metal object that had scraped inside my eye. After less than ten minutes, however, I did not feel any more pain or irritation. My eye, which could have been badly damaged, was completely healed! I took a closer look in the bathroom mirror to assess any potential injury. With amazing speed and overwhelming relief my eye had been completely healed through prayer that was commanded with an authority. The only remaining evidence of injury was redness still on my eye from the impact point of the bent antenna. I believe that was a reminder of His grace and glory that He had walked me through, as a testimony for others as well.

It doesn't surprise me that God prepares each of us to receive from Him. In times of suffering He catches our attention, so that at least we become willing to listen to Him. Remember, we are being transformed from glory to glory, and there is a transition in between each new level of glory that gets revealed to us, which is *suffering*. If you look at all the places in Scripture for suffering, it is almost always in the following pattern: suffering then glory. Although suffering is a temporary condition that has not been transformed by His glory yet. His loving choice is that He will not allow us to bear more than we can handle. "No temptation has overtaken you except such as is common to man; but God is faithful, who will not allow you to be tempted beyond what you are able, but with the temptation will also make the way of escape, that you may be able to bear it" (1 Corinthians 10:13 NKJV).

Beloved, do not think it strange concerning the fiery trial which is to try you, as though some strange thing happened to you; but rejoice to the extent that you partake of Christ's sufferings, that when His glory is revealed, you may also be glad with exceeding joy. If you are reproached for the name of Christ, blessed are you, for the Spirit of glory and of God rests upon you. On their part He is blasphemed, but on your part He is glorified. (1 Peter 4:12-14 NKJV)

22

Like the Garden of Eden

hen we have tasted and seen the manifestations of His glory, it instantly renews our thinking concerning His glory. It also rearranges our thinking because we know it was effortless on our part. We were just useful vessels for the Father to manifest His glory through us in spoken word form, not unlike how He also spoke words and things become. The story of the rich young ruler who spoke to Jesus reveals that even though he kept the commandments both outwardly and inwardly, he was not truly yielded to the voice of the Holy Spirit, evidenced by the Holy Spirit speaking through Jesus and the ruler not yielding. It had nothing to do with material wealth. The ruler received all that he did thus far by obeying the commandments. Jesus was about to unveil to him the intimate experiences in walking *with* Him in the Spirit; walking *with* Him in that spiritual realm called the Glory, being totally yielded.

So shall our days be as heaven upon the earth. Those who truly have this glory wisdom, this knowledge of His glory will proclaim and manifest the garden of Eden everywhere they go. They are taught with very private, intimate tutoring lessons by the Holy Spirit, exactly how to work with the Father, so that exactly how it is in heaven, so shall it be on earth.

If you look at something long enough it becomes appealing to you, this is true, but it is only one way that our eyes operate. "So when the woman saw that the tree was good for food, that it was pleasant to the eyes, and a tree desirable to make one wise, she took of its fruit and ate. She also gave to her husband with her, and he ate" (Genesis 3:6 NKJV). You begin to look at His promises, and they have become appealing to you. That desire for His word is how you know that His glory is becoming activated within you, and that is what will be manifested through you. It has become your desire. Your appeal for any one of His promises overcomes any other desire set before you. Is the appeal and desire for the Lord Jesus Christ more to you than the world we live in?

Yes, you can ask Him for anything, and when you ask, it is never necessary to place an *if* before it is His will, as in *if it is His will, such and such will* happen. We approach Him knowing emphatically that it is His promises we rely on, trust, and stand on confidently. His answer for every promise is YES, and through us, we just say AMEN! The amen is coming into alignment with the Father, which means, *"So be it, and let it be so in my life."*

My son, give attention to my words; Incline your ear to my sayings. Do not let them depart from your eyes; keep them in the midst of your heart; for they are life to those who find them, and health to all their flesh. (Proverbs 4:20-22 NKJV)

I had once been asked to pray specifically for employment to open up for someone. The couple was already working, but an opportunity for advancement arose, so they wanted prayer concerning that. I told them I was praying that not only would they get this promotion (they would be relocating to a different state) but also that their home would sell. After a few other needs were brought to my attention and I had committed to pray, a common response rose to the surface as the couple added, "If it is God's will, then it will happen. If not, then we will just reason that God didn't want us to move and have this promotion."

My reply was, "I believe we *never* have the authority to say, if it is Your will, unless we have droplets of blood on our face, (referring to Jesus praying in the garden). I do not have blood on my face; therefore, I can't say, '*If it is Your will.*'" I knew that it may have sounded a bit harsh, but I truly believe that we take all of His promises seriously and assertively. He has already given us total freedom to understand that every one of His promises are *Yes* in Christ, and through us, *Amen* is spoken to the glory of God. "For all the promises of God in Him *are* Yes, and in Him Amen, to the glory of God through us" (2 Corinthians 1:20 NKJV).

The second portion of the prayer request from the same people was concerning the sale of their home. Since the time they had first purchased the home, the economy had drastically changed, so now their home, which was at one time worth $180,000, had lost quite a bit in value and was now listed for only $135,000.

I asked directly, "How much do you want for the sale of the house?" I was told it was worth at least $180,000, but they did not expect to get that. I prayed and declared, "Go ministering angels, sell that house for more than $180,000. Thank you Father, in Jesus' name!" The house sold less than a month after this and in an economy when very few homes were being sold for $185,000. The news travelled quickly, for shortly after that, I was asked again to pray for someone else's home to sell.

I was asked to pray for the sale of another home, in which the first thing I asked, "How much do you want for it?" I was told like before that it was worth a lot more than what it was currently listed.

I asked again, "How much is it worth?"

The individual quickly said, "It is listed for only $240,000, but it was worth more than $300,000."

I asked again, "How much do you want for it?" I prayed the same as before, "Go ministering angels, sell this home for more than $300,000. Thank you Father, in Jesus' name!"

This home sold for $330,000 within about two weeks in an economy where very few homes were being sold.

We, as believers, choose to yield ourselves to the Holy Spirit. His influence dominates our thinking through the Word becoming one in our spirit. We can see these subtleties that are inherent in the heart of those around us, whether they are yielded to the Holy Spirit or not. If they have been driven and pushed along by evil spirits (that now dominate many lives) then what we view with *our* eyes is that structure (of darkness) being built into *their* lives. The spirit they have yielded to will show up quite naturally to our eyes.

For instance, if pride dominates a person, then behind-the-scenes in the spiritual realm, a spirit of pride has been influencing them. They have yielded themselves to it. Whether they are believers or unbelievers, it will still be obvious according to our insight. We have authority over all evil spirits; however, we still need to arrest their activity by using the authority that comes from the Father because we are in Christ. The truth from the Holy Spirit will stand out noticeably, because people listen to us. Those who do not listen have the truth filtered through the persistent pressure of other spirits. That is why the truth is still obscure to their hearts and minds. Influence from evil spirits has its greatest ability to sway in only people who have yielded themselves to those beings from the kingdom of darkness.

I am not referring to anyone's will, but rather to the negativity and dark activity surrounding and dominating their thoughts. It is distracting enough that evil spirits by their activity are able to influence people who do not listen and consequently people make poor choices, but this also drowns out any possibility of the truth from being clearly understood or perceived. This could be easily compared to a couple out on a date in a crowded venue with live music playing. The live music alone would cause enough distraction to make it difficult for them to hear each other. No matter how brilliant or insightful their language skills, words would have little to none effect in those conditions. There would be no quietness, no ability to carry on a genuine, intelligent conversation. The conversation would lack clarity, words and ideas would be missed. "You will keep him in perfect peace, whose mind is stayed on You, because he trusts in You" (Isaiah 26:3 NKJV).

Loud distractions also exist in the spiritual realm, which prevent others from hearing the truth. Take care of those distractions and you will make the truth available to others more easily, so that they can choose. Understand two things: We have authority in every realm by the name of Jesus. We understand the nature of this spiritual realm by every word from the Holy Spirit.

The words of a man's mouth are deep waters; The wellspring of wisdom is a flowing brook. (Proverbs 18:4 NKJV)

Counsel in the heart of man is like deep water, But a man of understanding will draw it out. (Proverbs 20:5 NKJV)

Deep calls unto deep at the noise of Your waterfalls; All Your waves and billows have gone over me. (Psalm 42:7 NKJV)

Jesus said, "...You shall love your neighbor as yourself" (Matthew 22:39 NKJV). It is clear that we need to learn to love ourselves, and it is growth that develops our ability to love Him more. He created you, and everything that He has created He called, "*Good.*" These are the words that reflect His heart, "That is Good!" You are just coming into alignment with what He already spoke.

As the Father loved Me, I also have loved you; abide in My love. (John 15:9 NKJV)

This is My commandment, that you love one another as I have loved you. (John 15:12 NKJV)

Do not love the world or the things in the world. If anyone loves the world, the love of the Father is not in him. (1 John 2:15 NKJV)

Already be aware that you will be given opportunity that will stretch your imagination and faith, so that the Holy Spirit can administer specific truths to your spirit. Truth makes its imprint deep within you, and will give you greater confidence with any new or similar circumstances. From one level of glory to the next, He keeps increasing the capacity for more faith in you to be released through your spoken words, which releases His glory.

The character and nature of the Father is expressed as *"nothing is impossible;"* however, this truth is not clearly understood throughout our experiences. The Holy Spirit is taking this truth and permeating it through our entire being until we are saturated with His glory—the *"nothing is impossible"* glory—which is not received through intellectual processes, but it comes in by revelation through our spirit. It has been His desire that we would experience very intimately as ONE—His glory in every imaginable way, so that we would manifest, *"nothing is impossible"*. That is the kind of glory that was operating in Jesus' ministry. He walked on water, fed the 5000, and power went out of Him to heal them all, as recorded by Luke.

And He came down with them and stood on a level place with a crowd of His disciples and a great multitude of people from all Judea and Jerusalem, and from the seacoast of Tyre and Sidon, who came to hear Him and be healed of their diseases, as well as those who were tormented with unclean spirits. And they were healed. And the whole multitude sought to touch Him, for power went out from Him and healed them all. (Luke 6:17-19 NKJV)

23

Showing Up For Practice

*R*eceive this revelation from the Holy Spirit deep within you. Expect that nothing is impossible. Expect that everything you say and declare manifests. This is what will begin to reflect from the Father, the revelation of His nature coming out through the words you speak. Through constant practice and perseverance these revelations are perfected in the things around us— whatever is not good, not acceptable, and not perfect because it is not the Father's will, becomes a *"glory experiment experience"* that gets transformed by the Father's divine nature in our words.

"Humble yourselves before the Lord, and he will exalt you" (James 4:10 ESV). Joseph told all of his brothers what he had dreamed, but they could not receive it, though it really was from the Father, and it manifested as He had revealed. The brothers meant to harm him for evil, but God meant it for good. "But as for you, you meant evil against me; but God meant it for good, in order to bring it about as it is this day, to save many people alive" (Genesis 50:20).

The expectation of the Father had revealed His glory being manifested through Joseph's life. That remains consistent with every child of light. He reveals to us amazing plans that could not possibly be achieved by our own impetus and then He ignites within our spirits the power to believe and act on His word.

At one point in my life I had attended a special music ministry that had been invited to our church; it also included a time of sharing testimonies of the Lord. This group of young people was a choir ensemble from another church. It is when they began speaking and sharing their testimonies that I had been affected the most. All of them had attended the same high school. What was revealed is that in the previous year there had only been a handful of Christians in their particular school. They decided that they wanted to see His glory manifested through the entire school, and began praying in agreement for that very thing.

The Word became contagious in their lives. They were no longer invisible but became outspoken, deliberately expressing their faith in the most natural means, but backed by God's extraordinary supernatural means. What began as only a mere handful of believers in the high school had increased to two-thirds of the whole student body being transformed in just one year. The attendance in this school was just over 900 students, so now there were over 600 newly born-again believers walking the halls.

This thought came to me, '*what He did in their school could happen in the high school in the town where I live.*'

This has to become a revelation from the Holy Spirit to be ignited with His promises. I talked with a good friend of mine, Ed, and expressed what I believed He wanted to do with the local high school. We did not know all that we would encounter, but we went with the *light* that had been revealed.

First, we went to the high school to visit and to check out what things were like in the spirit. This was not unlike how those twelve spies who were sent to check out the land they were going to conquer. We found student believers at the school and we visited with Christian teachers who we already knew. One thing we discovered, as it was being explained to us, was that every week between four to six students had been dropping out of school on average. This number seemed alarming. I think, though that it motivated us even more. (This truth I have written previously, "Whatever is not good, not acceptable, and not perfect is that place to begin using our faith to manifest His glory.")

We decided that we would get permission to go into the school during the lunch hour; as it was, we had total autonomy walking through the halls expressing to anyone willing to listen to simple things concerning Jesus. In those first few weeks we visited the high school two and three times per week. The few Christians we spoke with inside the school walls were reserved and said nothing to others about being believers. Our presence there made it possible for those believers to take a more open stand for Jesus in the midst of the school.

Once you begin walking in the direction the Holy Spirit leads, He reveals more *light* so that you gain wisdom for what else He has in mind. We had this kind of leading by Him, and then we went to all of the Bible-believing churches in the area to express our desires with the pastors of those churches. What the Holy Spirit had impressed upon us was a way that many churches would be linked together with what He wanted to do with these students from the high school. We told each of these pastors that God had directed us to open a door into the high school by encouraging and building up the believers who were already there and by being a visible demonstration of His love to others as we spoke to anyone who would listen.

Finally, it was our desire that each pastor we had spoken with would pray over our efforts, and specifically praying over a list we had compiled of all the youth from all these various churches. (This list included anyone who had ever been a part of their youth groups and attended the high school.) We encouraged these pastors to have those considered faithful in prayer in their respective congregations to pray over our list of young people. We just put feet to those prayers as the Holy Spirit gave directions in following His voice.

Almost immediately our visits paid off. The increase in the number of students that wanted to hear more about Jesus were more than we could effectively take time to discuss over any noon hour. We had a friend, Wayne, who had been leading a Bible study on Tuesday nights, so quite naturally we just invited those in the school to immediately act on their faith by attending the Bible study held on those nights.

In fact, we scheduled our visits to the school to only one day a week on Tuesdays so that it would coincide with the Bible study later in the evening. "He makes the whole body fit together perfectly. As each part does its own special work, it helps the other parts grow, so that the whole body is healthy and growing and full of love" (Ephesians 4:16 NLT).

The way in which the Holy Spirit was working through each person's life was uniquely orchestrated by Him. We just showed up for the *practices*. There were a lot of people who wanted Jesus in their lives. It was not particularly anything that we did, nor any special skill that we had possessed; it was mostly our enthusiasm about Jesus and our willingness to go where He was sending us.

And do not be conformed to this world, but be transformed by the renewing of your mind, that you may prove what *is* that good and acceptable and perfect will of God. (Romans 12:2 NKJV)

Looking at what has been described as the Great Commission, we can discover exactly how to disciple others through Jesus' own words to His disciples, "...teaching them to **observe** all that I have commanded you." From this whole discourse there are things to teach others to observe, such as "baptizing them in the name of the Father, and the Son, and the Holy Spirit" (Matthew 28:19-20). If we take a closer look at the word, "baptizing" we might momentarily state that as the word *immersing*. We should be teaching others how to observe being *immersed* in the Father's presence.

When Adam and Eve sinned, they knew they were naked and hid themselves from the Father's presence. The Father clothed them with animal skins after their fallen state. We, however, are blinded to the state of His glory when it comes to being clothed with Him. Mostly, the eyes of our understanding have not been enlightened to detect anything concerning His glory. We are to teach others how to **observe** and **detect** when they are clothed in His glory, versus when they are not.

We have taught others that when they received Christ they became a new creation and all things have become new; however, all that had truly taken place is that Christ is in us, the hope of glory. When we are **in Christ**, according to 2 Corinthians 5:17, that we are a new creation. We are created for glory. He forms us and He makes us.

The only place found in Scripture that uses this phrase, "Father of glory" is in Ephesians 1:17. "That the God of our Lord Jesus Christ, the Father of glory, may give to you the spirit of wisdom and revelation in the knowledge of Him." In this verse three different words reveal insight on the Father of glory: *wisdom*, *revelation*, and *knowledge*. *Wisdom* is the truth and framework found in Scripture. *Revelation* is every word that the Holy Spirit reveals to us. *Knowledge* is the permanent residency within us that Jesus described as His words abiding in us.

His glory is invisible, so we are clothed with that which is invisible. The Father has given us many images that are purposefully designed to capture the revelation of when we are clothed and when we are not. Hence, the direction given by the Holy Spirit,

> Casting down imaginations, and every high thing that exalteth itself against the knowledge of God, and bringing into captivity every thought to the obedience of Christ. (2 Corinthians 10:5 KJV)

Imaginations or images that are not in alignment with the knowledge of the glory do not clothe us with His glory. Only images that come from the Throne of Glory truly clothe us in His glory. For instance, from the Throne of Glory comes **perfect peace**. Anything that is not perfect peace is an image that will not clothe us in His glory. Instead, it is an image associated with *ripples on the pond* to be cast down.

> You will keep him in perfect peace, whose mind is stayed on You, because he trusts in You. (Isaiah 26:3 NKJV)

Riches of Glory

24

Yeast of Heaven

T here are certain components of His word that should be established in us. The truth should resonate within us, so that whatever it is we hear and see before us, we immediately know what to do. The training and guiding from the Holy Spirit who brought us to that place, activates what He has deposited in us. For example, He brings us to a community and asks, "Is there life in these dry bones?" He is using the question(s) as a catalyst to engage us in the truth that further establishes what He has deposited in us. We begin moving and operating in the knowledge of the glory. We are not just stating historical facts but intimately experiencing the same glory He and the Father have always known.

We become established in His glory—the divine nature—on one level, and from that level He stretches our imagination to continue walking in the Holy Spirit. He already knows what the glory in us will do, but we as yet do not, so He asks another simple question as a catalyst which moves us to listen more attentively so that we can start operating in what He reveals, "Can a nation be born in a day?" Practice fanning this now inside you, "What is the Holy Spirit telling you to do now?"

When it is revealed to you that Jesus is your Healer, you can see Him wearing that hat. Now you have access to what was always truth. It has been revealed to you in a way that you know that you know. Everything with Him is a past that has already become. Now when it becomes present tense it is not that you are going to get your healing. You were healed! That revelation must take place in the spirit for it to take root. Another example is to see Jesus seated in the heavenly places, but more accurately, to see you seated in the heavenly places with Him, so that you are able to manifest His glory in all things. This is not simply imagining that you are seated with Him. You intimately know that you are seated with Him *now*. You know that you have all of His authority in you *now*.

He is declaring to you, "You sit in the *Director's* chair!" You decide how this movie about *you* is going to be played out. You have His authority in you to make those kinds of choices. You see the end from the beginning. You know how the movie already ends. This glory releases the treasure that you already have within you. The abundance comes out in Word-form, filled with His glory, then acts as a catalyst that activates the changes you see through the words that you have spoken. The language of the Bible calls these words prayers of supplication when they are directed at the needs of all the saints.

You *decide* is a key word from the Father of glory. You *decide* that anything set before you is not even compared to the glory, which is radiating within you and is about to be revealed and released through your life in all that you say and do. Our hearts are surrendered willingly to Him; now our mouths become that efficacious instrument in the Father's design and plan for everyone that is called by His name. "For we are His workmanship, created in Christ Jesus for good works, which God prepared beforehand that we should walk in them" (Ephesians 2:10 NKJV).

These good works are the *glory fruit* that manifests through us. The wisdom and power of Jesus' life that flows through our words is a simple action: We pray with the expectation that everything we pray and say is manifested. We are one with Him. "And the glory which You gave Me I have given them, that they may be one just as We are one" (John 17:22 NKJV).

His glory is in the Tree of Life, while Words and Works are two of the Tree's branches. Fruit that is produced on these branches is Glory fruit. Our understanding of this revelation expresses its truth to our minds that the Words we speak and the Works we do produce glory fruit! If we were to hold them out in a balance scale—they weigh the same. The Father has declared that He hates dishonest scales. His Words and His Works have the same weight in the spirit. We capture this revelation by just speaking His words. Jesus knows that our ability to operate in the spiritual realm will accelerate our understanding when we speak His words, so that we can truly agree with what the psalmist declared, "Taste and see that the Lord is good" (Psalm 34:8).

Those who had observed Jesus, the Son of Man, asked the very curious question that we too should be asking, "When He had come to His own country, He taught them in their synagogue, so that they were astonished and said, 'Where did this Man get this wisdom and these mighty works?'" (Matthew 13:54 NKJV). Where did He get this wisdom and mighty works? The indirect answer to where Jesus received His authority is when He said, *either believe the words I speak or the works I do, for it is the Father in Me doing the works* (John 10:37-38; 14:10,11, paraphrase mine). Jesus is giving us a complete picture of how the glory operates in Him, and how this same glory operates in us. The Father uses honest scales; therefore, the knowledge of the glory—His words—weigh the same as the manifestation of the glory. Hence, the more we receive revelation from the Holy Spirit *about* His glory, the more that glory produces manifestations. His word in us is fused with His glory; the two are not separate.

This higher walk corresponds directly with all the complications of knowing this higher math, of knowing what ONE really means. By the tutoring of the Holy Spirit, we turn the page to discover it was never complicated. In order to direct our hearts, transform our thoughts, and guide our footsteps, Jesus said, "He who eats My flesh and drinks My blood abides in Me, and I in him" (John 6:56 NKJV). "And the glory which You gave Me I have given them, that they may be one just as We are one" (John 17:22 NKJV).

Communion is not just our entrance, but it is the simplest form of prayer, meditation, and worship. The Holy Spirit begins to unveil the hidden truths, the deep revelations that have been stored within His heart, in the same way that there have been deep revelations stored within our own heart. Both hearts have suffered and manifested glory, for it is the Father's heart that is revealed. If you have suffered, you have come to understand more from Love's perspective just how Jesus had suffered. The suffering is shared, but the glory, which He has enjoyed, is also shared. We are learning this language of the glory through the following equation and language of communion: I abide in you and you abide in Me.

The language of this *glory equation* is resolved and understood by the Professor, the Holy Spirit Himself. He has been operating in the glory since before the beginning of time. He is teaching the exact equation of His glory, which we are able to understand through covenant. He reveals small bites at a time so that the simplicity in Christ is not overshadowed by the depth of wisdom from the Father. At the end of a week in class with the Holy Spirit teaching, He asks a pop quiz question, "Can these dry bones live?" No matter what question He asks, it is intended to be presented to stretch our imaginations around the idea of His awakened glory within us, so that His glory can be useful to meet the demand of any negative condition for the purpose of manifesting and transforming that condition. That is the awesome beauty of being One with Him. Without Him we can do nothing, but with Him, nothing is impossible. This is the kind of glory He has deposited within us, the *nothing is impossible* glory.

Here is the *glory equation* spelled out in the transitive property of equality. If A = B and if B = C then A = C since things equal to the same thing (B) are equal to each other. It is a self-evident truth that things which are equal to the same thing are equal to each other. If the Glory is equal to the Holy Spirit, and if the Holy Spirit is equal to yeast, then the Glory is equal to yeast.

The Glory is equal to the Holy Spirit by the Father's own definition. The Word says that the Holy Spirit raised Jesus from the dead, "But if the Spirit of Him who raised Jesus from the dead dwells in you, He who raised Christ from the dead will also give life to your mortal bodies through His Spirit who dwells in you" (Romans 8:11 NKJV). And also it declares that the Glory of the Father raised Jesus from the dead, "Therefore we were buried with Him through baptism into death, that just as Christ was raised from the dead by the glory of the Father, even so we also should walk in newness of life" (Romans 6:4 NKJV).

The Holy Spirit was poured out on Pentecost, identifying with this Feast in the same way that Jesus was the Lamb of God who took away the sin of the world, identifying with the Passover Feast. Out of all the Feasts of Israel, yeast was only used in the Feast of Pentecost. So we can see that both the Holy Spirit and yeast are identified in the Pentecost Feast. According to our glory equation, since *Glory* is equal to the *Holy Spirit* in the Resurrection, and the *Holy Spirit* is equal to identifying with *yeast* in the Pentecost Feast, then the *Glory* is equal to identifying with *yeast*.

The proof is even more astounding when you compare that with what Jesus had to say about yeast and glory. Concerning yeast, "...The kingdom of heaven is like the yeast a woman used in making bread. Even though she put only a little yeast in three measures of flour, it permeated every part of the dough" (Matthew 13:33 NLT).

Then more precisely concerning the glory (used as a noun), "And the glory which You gave Me I have given them, that they may be one just as We are one" (John 17:22 NKJV). The activity of the glory makes us one. The activity of the yeast makes the flour one. It rises, permeates, saturates, and makes as one.

Let's look again at the language of the Father (which Jesus had already declared) *Man shall not live by bread alone, but by every Word that proceeds from the mouth of God.* We should understand that everything the Holy Spirit speaks is extremely important. These three verses in Scripture should mark our minds concerning the Resurrection, Romans 8:11, 1 Corinthians 6:14, and Romans 6:4. All of them deal with the language of the Father concerning this one aspect, which is the resurrection of the Lord Jesus Christ.

The Father's wisdom is expressed in every word. He took three different words to describe the single-most important event in all of history—the resurrection of the Lord Jesus Christ. Those words He revealed are all on the same plate— Holy Spirit, power, and glory—and are found in these verses: Romans 8:11, 1 Corinthians 6:14, and Romans 6:4, respectively. The more we have revelation from the Holy Spirit, the more we have direct wisdom concerning His power, and knowledge of His glory, and vice versa.

If we ask ourselves, "What do I know about the Holy Spirit?" One thing we know is that the Holy Spirit was poured out on the Day of Pentecost. But what do we really know about Pentecost? The same way that Jesus identified with Passover as the Lamb of God who takes away the sin of the world, the Holy Spirit is identified with Pentecost. There is one simple aspect that we can discover about the Pentecost Feast: it is the ONLY Feast that is celebrated with bread that contains yeast. Why?

Jesus called Himself the *Bread of Life*. We miss the depth of wisdom from the Holy Spirit if the dots are not connected. Jesus said "Beware of the yeast of the Pharisees", though He NEVER said, "Beware of the yeast of heaven." Yeast of heaven? Where is that? In Matthew 13:33 Jesus said, "…The kingdom of heaven is like the yeast a woman used in making bread. Even though she put a little yeast in three measures of flour, it permeated every part of the dough." He tells us exactly what heaven is like. It is like yeast. Now we know we have direct access to understanding more about the Feast of Pentecost, in which the Holy Spirit has identified.

Once again, let's examine by reviewing what Scripture has already revealed by listing them together for our eyes to see the Father's wisdom concerning the Resurrection;

the Holy Spirit raised Jesus from the dead
(Romans 8:11);

the power of God raised Jesus from the dead
(1 Corinthians 6:14);

the glory of the Father raised Jesus from the dead
(Romans 6:4);

and if we remind ourselves of what Jesus said about Himself
—I am the Bread of Life, then we can accurately say the
yeast of heaven raised the Bread of Life. This truth marks
our mind forever. It renews our thinking to understand why
and how the Father has used three different words to
describe the most important event in all of history. Jesus not
only called Himself, the *Bread of Life,* but even the name of
His birthplace, Bethlehem, means house of bread. Jesus
really has been destined to bring us the New Covenant.
Reflect on what He said about communion, "...as often as
you do this, do in remembrance of Me." It is unveiling more
about His glory, so that you can say accurately when taking
communion, "I am reminding my mind that Christ, the Living
Bread, is in me. He is the hope of glory that is about to be
revealed through my life in all that I say and do."

25

Glory's Unlimited Potential

*I*magine everyone you meet has this unlimited potential of His glory manifesting through them. Now imagine that the Holy Spirit is already working with them to bring that to fruition, and that He has sent you to engage them in any way to help propagate that which He has already begun. You are simply using discernment to determine where you need to begin and what it is that you might say. In this way, the greatest amount of revelation that is already within them will be ignited by your words. The ministry of reconciliation is using words of reconciliation to give an accurate accounting of His glory that is being manifested through you in the domain in which He has placed you.

There remains a certain amount of excitation and joy within us when we do perceive and discern the spiritual conditions present, whether few or many. This allows us to begin working with Him on this unique assignment to which we have been sent. The ministry of the Holy Spirit has been advancing and preparing the way before us. There is now much anticipation from all of creation, which is anxiously waiting to see the works of His glory manifesting through us. Jesus said, *either believe the words I say, or believe the works I do, for it is the Father in Me doing the works.* These are two of the branches or arteries from the main stream in His glory. When received, they transform any condition by the words and works that He has activated within us.

You are reading *Riches of Glory* by righteous decree, for He has ordered your steps. And all the treasuries of His wisdom are being revealed and fed to you by the Holy Spirit. The prophet Elijah had been fed by the ravens, but he was also fed food given to him by angels. Your food from the Holy Spirit is prepared as a special diet suited to your needs exclusively. No one else knows you as intimately as the Holy Spirit. He is very much acquainted with all your sorrows and joys. He grieves with the same grief that you have endured. In that you have suffered with Him, He suffers with you. Everything you experience, He experiences with you. You can rejoice knowing that if you suffer for His sake, you also enjoy His glory. It is through the suffering that His Glory is revealed in you.

When we take communion it is a mutually enjoyed experience knowing He has suffered and knowing He knows we have suffered. He does not leave the shared experiences with only that we have suffered, because He also creates for us the joy of intimately experiencing His glory in all that is set before us. This is an amazing love and definitely victorious in every way, so that Jesus' own words, "Gather up the fragments that none be lost", becomes a living reality to all who have ever suffered, as the pieces of their lives begin to come together and make sense.

All of us who have been fragmented by this world's system have this to look forward to, "You are of God, little children, and have overcome them, because He who is in you is greater than he who is in the world" (1 John 4:4). We are more than conquerors through Christ. Today we taste that victory time and time again. Every time we take communion we are reminded of that death-defeating glory is in us. We are ignited in the midst of the trials with the passionate words of the Holy Spirit. He strengthens us and causes us to rise to the occasion. His wisdom is revealed and we have perfect confidence in His unfailing love that is being released to us, through us, and for us.

Imagine, if you will, that Jesus went on vacation and left us with His glory in us. He also left us with the Holy Spirit to teach us how to operate and work with Him in manifesting His glory while He was away. The power of His glory is capable of doing any thing. Now imagine Jesus coming back from vacation to find everything in disarray and out of order. Wouldn't He be able to ask, "What did you do with My glory?" What works on a smaller scale is also the potency that works on a grander scale. He has assigned us to a specific realm, which includes all the people who cross our paths every day, to refine us in operating in His glory.

When Jesus was in the grave, a bad economy did not wake Him up from the grave. Things getting worse did not wake Him from the grave. The evil in high places in every segment of society did not wake Him from the grave. It was the glory of the Father that raised Jesus from the grave. We are His body, and what will wake us from the grave is the same glory of the Father. The nature of His glory not only awakens us but also empowers us to bring about the changes He desires. The Holy Spirit is completely desirous to bring us up higher in experience, wisdom, and power. The signature of walking and working with Him in His glory is what has sealed us. "Therefore we were buried with Him through baptism into death, that just as Christ was raised from the dead by the glory of the Father, even so we also should walk in newness of life" (Romans 6:4 NKJV).

Anything that is not His nature in us is a stronghold that must be exposed to this divine nature by the use of His word. "For though we walk in the flesh, we do not war according to the flesh. For the weapons of our warfare are not carnal but mighty in God for pulling down strongholds, casting down arguments and every high thing that exalts itself against the knowledge of God, bringing every thought into captivity to the obedience of Christ, and being ready to punish all disobedience when your obedience is fulfilled" (2 Corinthians 10:3-6 NKJV).

On our radar within us, anything that does not accurately express His nature, either in thought, emotion, or action is a stronghold that has not been systematically dealt with and put in its place. The words that describe the process of how we are working together with the Holy Spirit to perfect the nature of Christ in us by **pulling**, **casting**, **bringing**, and **being**, are expressed by God like this:

Pulling — removing anything that hinders our ability to perceive that we are sitting on the Throne of Glory with Christ. We are pulling down strongholds, removing all doubt that we are seated with Him on this Throne.

Casting — throwing out and downward everything that exalts itself against this knowledge of the glory. The glory is pre-eminent. It is above all the heavens and the earth. The knowledge of God is the knowledge of His glory.

Bringing — willingly search the source of every thought to align with His thoughts. We bring the sacrifice, the fruit of our lips with thanksgiving to Christ.

Being — we are new creations, supernatural beings created in Christ. We use our authority to destroy destructive free radicals. Once we have a settled foundation in any one area of our lives, we also have received the victory in that area, e.g., where there is sickness, we now have health; nothing except health is acceptable to us, so we now transform the conditions wherever sickness is running rampant.

Dead works come from the old nature. If His glory is not being manifested, it is a dead work. Those dead works are strongholds which have not yet yielded to the wisdom of the Holy Spirit. We should not only expect that what we declare will manifest supernatural results, but also that it is a change that lasts. "You did not choose Me, but I chose you and appointed you that you should go and bear fruit, and that your fruit should remain, that whatever you ask the Father in My name He may give you" (John 15:16 NKJV).

What is meant by fruit? The answer to this question can be found in the verse we just read. We ask the Father by the authority of Jesus' name and it opens the flow of His glory. The fruit is a direct result of the life that is in the vine. His word is filled with His glory. Jesus had already said that apart from Him we can do nothing. Now Jesus is revealing the distinctive nature of what kind of fruit. Not just manifesting fruit, which is important, but manifesting fruit that has eternal implications, because His word is eternal. It is His word in us that is radiating with His glory and coming out of our lives in everything we say and do.

This is the exact pattern that Jesus declared about Himself, *I only do what I see the Father doing, I only say what I hear the Father speaking, and apart from the Father I can do nothing.* (John 5:19,20; 8:28; 12:49,50) Jesus makes an amazing statement in John 14:11 as to how this fruit is manifested, "Believe Me that I am in the Father and the Father in Me, or else believe Me for the sake of the works themselves (the Father in Jesus is doing the works.)" The pattern for us is that Christ is in us, which is good, but even better than that, we are in Christ. Without that second spiritual connection the heavenly wiring is not complete. And if not complete then there is no power manifesting His glory through us. The fruit is the words and the works that are being manifested through us.

The language of the New Covenant is expressed in terms like this, "He abides in Me and I abide in Him." For us to abide in Him we are already partaking of the glory; now expect supernatural results from the words we speak. We take on the role as ambassadors, directly expressing the authority from the Throne of Glory. Jesus said, "Nevertheless I tell you the truth. It is to your advantage that I go away; for if I do not go away, the Helper will not come to you; but if I depart, I will send Him to you" (John 16:7 NKJV). Has it been considered and thoroughly understood as to why Jesus could not have sent the Holy Spirit unless He had gone to be with the Father? We are able to understand the simplicity of this through our filter of His glory wisdom: Jesus sent His word to heal the centurion's servant. When we come up higher in how the Father is thinking, we realize the ability to send the Holy Spirit is far above just sending His word. He is sending the very presence of the glory of the Father—the Holy Spirit, the very Spirit of Glory. Jesus is sitting on the Throne of Glory releasing the highest level of glory imaginable—the Spirit of Glory.

The language of the New Covenant is also expressed as *greater works*. Jesus declared, "he who believes in Me, the works that I do he will also do." That is the language of an Old Covenant Man filled with the Holy Spirit. He then said, "And greater works than these will he do, because I go to the Father." These *greater works* are being manifested through New Covenant believers who are filled with the Holy Spirit. There are no limitations in His glory. The limitations only remain in our thoughts that have not yet been surrendered or yielded to Him. They have not yet been transformed by the power of the Holy Spirit. We work with the Holy Spirit when we bring each thought captive that is contrary to any promises, and we cast it off as dead works.

Have you ever wondered why Jesus said, "...and greater works than these he will do, because I go to My Father" (John 14:12 NKJV)? What He said is so profound that it seems almost unimaginable to conceive of; it would be without our relationship with and the help we have from the Holy Spirit. Jesus equates our ability to operate in those *greater works* by simply knowing that He is with the Father. Again in the book of John, chapter 16, we learn that it is the Holy Spirit's ministry and work to reveal this truth, "...of righteousness, because I go to My Father and you see Me no more" (John 16:10 NKJV). These two truths unfold the mystery about operating in the *greater works*. The Holy Spirit's work in our lives sometimes goes unnoticed. Here in this particular case, the evidence for the reason we know that Jesus went to the Father is from the work of the Holy Spirit. He has performed *laser-light* surgery on our hearts so that we have no difficulty knowing this is truth.

Father, we thank you for such profound wisdom that You continuously reveal. We trust You to perfect within us all that is lacking in our understanding of all Your ways and all Your thoughts. We totally thank you that Jesus died, justified, and satisfied all the requirements for us to now live in Your presence and glory that You have chosen we would enjoy. We receive Your Holy Spirit's direction in our lives. We value all that You say and have given as our New Covenant. We understand that we do not have Your whole counsel and are interdependent on one another. We ask that You remind us always to be peaceable, submitted to one another, and choosing to walk in love always. Faithfully, You watch over all of our ways. We thank you with the Love You have placed in our hearts, which is Your own dear Love that You have for Jesus. Empower us now with Your glory in all that we say and do to reflect all that You desire in order to show Yourself mighty, in Jesus' name Amen!

26

Paid in Full

He is teaching us on the glory, and all those whom He is teaching, He is expecting a return on His investment. He expects now that we are being taught by the Holy Spirit, so it has become our responsibility to wake up the body of Christ. Even if we were the only ones in the whole world, we are now responsible for the whole world, but we begin with the body of Christ. "Therefore, as we have opportunity, let us do good to all, especially to those who are of the household of faith" (Galatians 6:10 NKJV). When He comes back will He find faith? Will He find those He has taught on this knowledge of the glory using what they now know? He has declared to us that His glory is greater, because it *is* greater. The practical application is for His glory to be manifested in every realm of this earth. "For the earth will be filled with the knowledge of the glory of the Lord, as the waters cover the sea" (Habakkuk 2:14 NKJV).

Upon hearing the confirmation of the Holy Spirit, we can ask our Father, "How can I be part of what You are doing Father to wake up the body of Christ worldwide? What is it that You have assigned to me personally, so that I can come into alignment with the leading of the Holy Spirit? I come to You willingly to be Your yielded vessel of honor and glory. I thank You that You are confirming now in my heart and mind that I have been given a specific task and appointment to manifest fruit that will remain. Here I am, help me be part of this vision that You have given these brothers and sisters in Christ at Streams of Glory. With supplicating prayers supplying all the needs, spirit, soul, and body, I totally commit my heart, soul, and body to develop in agreement with the prophetic message that You have imparted to us. Amen!" If this is you, move in the exact direction in which the Holy Spirit is speaking to you now. Thank you in Jesus' name!

If those of us who have this treasure were well aware of how powerful His glory is in us, we would not protest. We would execute precise action to manifest His glory. He has given us executive privilege and power to do so. "His intent was that now, through the church, the manifold wisdom of God should be made known to the rulers and authorities in the heavenly realms" (Ephesians 3:10 NIV). The genetic engineering by the Father has taken place in the life of Jesus. All that has been imparted into Christ's life is being manifested into our lives, simply by us yielding ourselves to the Holy Spirit.

The yielded state is the true nature of the disciple. It comes in higher than the language of obedience. Being yielded rearranges how we think, decide, and express any emotion. It is what directs, sends, and empowers the true disciple; it is the very heartbeat of the voice of the Holy Spirit. If it has not been birthed in us, then it is not imparted to others. In the same way Jesus was sent, we too, are being sent. We are empowered by our assertiveness with the Holy Spirit to follow Him accurately in the simplest of details without always trying to analyze, reason, or feel good about it first. Most of the time God will lead us to a place that it is deliberately uncomfortable but not without His private tutoring and specialized training created specifically for us. The results glorify the Father because of that yielded state with the Holy Spirit.

He has placed all those things around us in nature to give us a total understanding that rises above the beauty and sees the wisdom from the Father. As children of the light, all things that have been created have an appointed time in which we manifest His glory. We are growing up to be like Christ with the understanding and knowing that the whole of creation is anxiously waiting for what He placed within us to be released through our spoken words. To be intimate with the Father is to know the Master's business. "Now I say that the heir, as long as he is a child, does not differ at all from a slave, though he is master of all, but is under guardians and stewards until the time appointed by the father. Even so we, when we were children, were in bondage under the elements of the world" (Galatians 4:1-3 NKJV).

What takes place in us when we no longer think and act as a child, begins to thrill the imagination so much with all of the possibilities that are set before us. The Scripture above declares that as children we are still under bondage to the elements of this world. When we are no longer acting as a child spiritually, then we are no longer in bondage to the elements of this world. The realm in which the Lord of glory walked was above the elements of the world. He was not under bondage to any of the laws of physics or science. He gives us a thorough look, a clear view into the supernatural realm in which He has authorized us to walk in as well.

The spirit to spirit language and communication is pure and filled with peace. It is this communication of which your spirit desires to taste all that He desires. The reason why you have allowed the Word to have its place in your heart is because He has fulfilled the longing within it. He has chosen that His Word would satisfy completely. "Sanctify them by Your truth. Your word is truth. And for their sakes I sanctify Myself, that they also may be sanctified by the truth" (John 17:17,19 NKJV). There is another verse that says it this way, "Deep calls unto deep at the noise of Your waterfalls; all Your waves and billows have gone over me" (Psalm 42:7 NKJV). You know what He is like now through every word the Holy Spirit declares to you. Each word is building upon a foundation that He has already established within you. We have enough light to walk now in simple glimpses of His glory, so here is our assignment: I challenge anyone who wants to taste and see that the Lord is good. We are forming a unique opportunity to manifest His glory through answered prayers. Make your prayers known, no matter what the degree of difficulty is in your mind. Together we are going to taste and see how good the Lord truly is.

I had received a letter from the IRS a couple of years ago stating that I owed them $17,000 in taxes. I had a CPA who had already handled my taxes for the year in question. It is true I did owe for that particular year but far less than what the IRS had said. I took my papers and placed them in an envelope. I was inspired by the Holy Spirit in the moment, so I wrote on my envelope, PAID IN FULL, IN JESUS' NAME! Then I mailed the letter.

A couple of months later I received another letter from the IRS, stating that now I owed $16,500 and small change, because they had taken money from my payroll check to pay off what they declared I owed. My reaction was to speak to the letter, "I called *you* paid for in full in Jesus' name," and tossed the letter on the table. Three weeks later I received another letter from the IRS. This time $13,000 had been dismissed and I only owed $4,000. My reaction was consistent, "I call you paid in full, in Jesus' name!" A month later I received another letter from the IRS; this time they *owed me* $231.92 and my debt to them had been completely dismissed!

Relating to the common thread that binds every truth concerning His glory, each word from the Holy Spirit is establishing a greater understanding in the spiritual realm. He, not only gives us keen understanding, but He also takes each *pearl* and sets it within a whole string of *pearls* that consists of wisdom and experiences. The balance in the Father's heart includes both the revelation of His glory and the experiences of His glory. His purpose for us is to have such a sound foundation in our wisdom and knowledge of

His glory, so that we have immediate revelation when some new adventure is awakened before us. This new task is aimed at creating a greater reality, a deeper intimate experience in Christ. These simple truths that were once known have expanded into all kinds of possibilities in Him. That is why Jesus said, "...When you lift up the Son of Man, then you will know that I am He, and that I do nothing of Myself; but as My Father taught Me, I speak these things" (John 8:28 NKJV).

27

Giving Glory to the Father

D o you see Christ seated on the Throne of Glory or only being lifted up on the cross? How we see Jesus truly makes a difference in our own spiritual understanding, because how we see Him develops where the Holy Spirit is leading us. We will grow most assuredly by every word from the Holy Spirit. He is being assertive in our ability to experience what Jesus had prayed in John 17:5 "And **now**, O Father, glorify Me together with Yourself, with the glory which I had with You **before** the world was." You will notice that Jesus is talking about two different times: the BEFORE and the NOW. We live with Him *now*. The image of Him is what we should have of Him *now*. Jesus is the same yesterday, today, and forever, but it is also true that we are becoming what He is *now*. That change is taking place in us through what the Holy Spirit reveals to us. What is this *now* image in our experiences? We are seated with Christ *now* in the heavenly realms.

He was glorified together with the Father, and it is the glory that glorified them together. This same glory is what glorifies us together with Him. We are ONE with Him. That image of ONE with Him is *now*. The Father's good purposes for our lives were always this way. He already had an image of what we are like in Christ. He already knew what that image would be like, for He is ONE with the Son. The Father is in Jesus, and Jesus is in the Father. That same image is what is true in us. We must see ourselves in all this truth, not just *Christ in us*. We must see that *we are in Him* as well. That is how He is with the Father, glorified together with Him. They are glorified together with the glory; we are glorified together with the glory.

This wisdom of His glory in us and us in His glory is the good news concerning all that He has for us. Jesus glorified together with the Father is the relationship in the glory that we share together. The Father has already chosen that we would be conformed to Christ's image. It is the image of His glory in us, which He called us to receive. We are purchased by His Blood and glorified together with Him. We enter this relationship purified by His Blood, so that the relationship glorifies the Father. Jesus lived and walked with the Father in Him, and He in the Father. There is no darkness in Him. That is what He chose our experiences to be; no darkness in us at all. Glory reigns in us!

They [the Godhead] said, "Let Us make man in Our image." We are made in the image of the second Adam. The enemy knows the power of the second Adam and was defeated. For this purpose the second Adam is manifested.

Every time we manifest His glory, it destroys the works of the enemy. We look with delight into this image that we are *now* in Christ, and we are transformed. This image in us is the radiating glory of the Father. Without Jesus we would not have this image alive in us. We know the image we had *before* Christ; we have a new image *now*, and the new image purifies us *now*. The Father chose us to be conformed to this image; we are being purified, not mixed with any other image *now*. The full manifestation of His glory in us is glorious. This same image is what glorifies the Father and is the fullness of His glory.

It refreshes our hearts to know Him, to know His word, and to know His word is truth. This refreshing gives the weary rest. We have His Spirit in us. We are free to operate with His authority and follow His leading, to walk in His glory with the same delight in which He walks in His glory. We walk with Him and are delighted that His glory transforms, purifies, and refreshes us.

He is the Healer, we are transformed into health.

As He is, so are we. We have His image, His glory in us *now* in this world.

His pure word from heaven finishes and completes us. We are glorified together with Him. His pure word is filled with His glory.

We have peace, because He is peace.

We have His word living in us.

His word is filled with His glory.

He is the Word.

He is the Lord of Glory.

We have become glorified together with Him, we are one with Him *now*.

Giving glory back to the Father is the deepest expression of love that we can give to Him, and it makes perfect sense to be able to please Him like never before when we understand these words from the Holy Spirit. It is about giving glory to Him in every way and in every area! To walk in love, to walk this out, is setting the body of Christ in a whole new realm and taking back tremendous territory that the enemy has stolen, namely marriages; the thief brought divorce into the church that is many times at a higher rate than in the world.

You have asked Jesus to come into your life; now step into His life. He walks with you, and you walk with Him. The Father is in Me, and I am in the Father. Let those words resonate in you. He has established you to have the same Life that He has; that image where the Father is in you, and you are in the Father. It is new to you to be introduced to the Father. Teach your mouth to give praises to the Father and to speak the Father's words.

Man shall not live by bread alone, but by every word
that proceeds from the mouth of God. (Matthew 4:4)

You believe in Jesus, this is very good. I am saying now,
IN HIM (Christ) believe. Do your believing for any promise
while you are IN HIM. The imagination must realize that you
are IN HIM. You have the Father's love speaking to you. His
love has been shed abroad in your heart. You are so
covered by His Love for you that you are loved in the same
way He loves Jesus. The revelation that you are loved as
much as He loves Jesus comes alive and has its deepest
experiences when you begin to pray. You know that you
have what you ask for when you know He loves you and
answers your prayer as quickly as He answers Jesus'
prayers. Hear yourself saying, "I thank you Father that You
always hear me. I thank you Father for Your favor. I thank
you Father for Your wisdom."

Say, Christ in me, in whom I am well pleased. I am
pleased to manifest the Father's glory through Christ. Amen!
He is speaking to you so that you understand all that you
see before you is only a temporary status. You are learning
about His glory and how this glory operates in you. You are
actually at the crossroads where things are being changed
by Him through you. You may fine-tune with this language of
prayer, "I thank You for Your glory that You have given to me.
I thank You for the spiritual realm You have assigned to me. I
ask that You give me wisdom to bring peace wherever I go
and to overflow with joy under any condition. Thank you,
Father for gracing my life with tremendous favor and
wisdom. In Jesus' mighty name. Amen!"

We, however, will not boast beyond measure, but within the limits of the sphere which God appointed us—a sphere which especially includes you… not boasting of things beyond measure, that is, in other men's labors, but having hope, that as your faith is increased, we shall be greatly enlarged by you in our sphere, (2 Corinthians 10:13,15 NKJV)

Then this Daniel distinguished himself above the governors and satraps, because an excellent spirit was in him; and the king gave thought to setting him over the whole realm. (Daniel 6:3 NKJV)

Then the realm of Jehoshaphat was quiet, for his God gave him rest all around. (2 Chronicles 20:30 NKJV)

Notice in the previous Scriptures in block quote how they reveal to us that God has appointed each of us an entire realm in which to operate with Him in His glory. We each have our own *sandbox* to practice in with the Holy Spirit until that whole realm is transformed by His glory. He has already chosen in advance that we would go from glory to glory as a promotion in the spirit. Hence, the promise given by Jesus our Lord in the book of Revelation, "And he who overcomes, and keeps My works until the end, to him I will give power over the nations" (Revelation 2:26 NKJV).

The Father's purpose from before time began was to live in intimate fellowship with us and that we would always enjoy His presence in our lives. The plan of salvation was never *Plan B*, nor was it a reaction to what took place in the

Garden of Eden. 2 Thessalonians 2:14 expresses the whole purpose of the gospel, which is for obtaining the glory of the Lord Jesus Christ. What we received when we first ask Christ into our lives is His glory. His glory is deposited within all those who call on His name; however, initially it is inactive and dormant. Hence, the Scripture declares, "Christ in you, the hope of glory." While His glory is in all those who are in covenant relationship with Jesus, we still need to awaken His glory as the psalmist said, "Wake up My glory!"

We receive wisdom, revelation, and knowledge of the glory from the Holy Spirit. It is so essential to the growth of every believer to be transformed from being just a believer to becoming a disciple. We must be disciplined in the skills of listening and following the voice of the Holy Spirit and learning how to work with Him in His glory. All the miracles that Jesus did were performed by the Father in Him. This was the glory of the Father working in Him. Jesus gave us the same glory that He received so that we would also experience the same glory to perform all the mighty works of the Father through us. Our promotions in the spirit are based upon the ability to continue manifesting His glory in all we say and do!

28

The Table Is Set

U niquely hear these words from the Master, "If you forgive the sins of any, they are forgiven them; if you retain the sins of any, they are retained" (John 20:23 NKJV). Jesus has given us a ministry of reconciliation, a ministry to restore. He restored the glory, now we restore His glory wherever we go. We are appointed as ambassadors using words of reconciliation and words to restore. We have greater authority from walking in His peace, and definitely we are not mimicking the same words of this world. We walk in joy, and this joy is what we impart to others (not some kind of Christian philosophy), but we are releasing life!

Expect a hunger that you have never known and a sphere that is broken through that only He could have done. We simply walk through that envelope of His glory that will effortlessly radiate out of all those who intimately follow the voice of the Holy Spirit. You can expect a miracle in any one thing that you believe God for. That attitude should be deeply engrained in the core of your being. This is more of an awareness than anything else, since Jesus already said,

"...Have faith in God" (Mark 11:22 NKJV). I have much testimony where others have asked me to pray concerning any particular need. I totally trust Him to answer my prayer, for others especially. He teaches us how to stir each other's faith, so that we create an atmosphere around us that is contagious with His glory.

Every example for answered prayer should be expressed in the midst of the *storm* no matter how it measures with our own thinking. One person asked me if God could restore their jewelry that had been stolen. It was worth over $10,000. I had declared with an assertiveness, "Go ministering angels, cause the jewelry to be restored completely." This person asked, "Are we going to pray?" I said, "I have already declared it!" I took time to pray also for their benefit. Four months later all the jewelry that had been stolen was completely returned—nothing was missing.

We connect with Him in His glory, and He continues to confirm again and again that nothing is too difficult for Him. Jesus once said how the Father was revealing to Him the wisdom from heaven, "When you lift up the Son of Man, then you will know that I am He, and that I do nothing of Myself; but as My Father taught Me, I speak these things" (John 8:28 NKJV). When we confess and speak up about Jesus before men, He is faithful to confess us before the Father. Now you place His words in your mouth to taste and see how good they really are.

The term *joint-heirs* means that everything He received, we, likewise receive. The inheritance is only valid if Jesus has died, for only then is the inheritance given. We know that He died. We also know that He was given the glory. He was crowned with glory. This is not a crown that is worn on His head, but He is completely surrounded by the glory. It is His armor of light that we bear.

"Whose minds the god of this age has blinded, who do not believe, lest the light of the gospel of the glory of Christ, who is the image of God, should shine on them" (2 Corinthians 4:4 NKJV). This verse says that Jesus received the good news of the glory, "...the image of God" shining on (Him). We receive this *image* as well. It is the image of the new creation. Everything we need is already in us. It is manifested out of us through His words in us that are spoken. Through constant use and practice we are perfecting the language of the spirit. This is not trial and error; it is the release of His glory in near impossible conditions as understood by our minds. Each manifestation of His glory perfects our thinking.

His Rhema word is impregnated with His glory. We say *shine on* us, but the reality is this light is radiating, penetrating, and permeating our entire being 'til we are saturated with it in our thoughts, our emotions, and our wills. One word from Him totally transforms us because it is Life and Spirit; it is a life-giving, life-imparting, supernatural word. Take His word and allow it to go to the core of your being. Jesus said that He came that we might have life and have life more abundantly. The word that the Holy Spirit makes known to us, even if only one verse, is Life. It is the same word that Jesus gave, which is being deposited within us.

The overflow of that Life is the image of His glory, not only in us, but now all around us as the armor of light. The light that *shines in* us, now becomes the light *shining on* and all around us. His glory is first activated within us, then it rises up and beams forth from us.

We are being glorified together with Him with the leading of the Holy Spirit and by following His voice even through those tough areas that we consider suffering. It is not a suffering FOR the Lord; it is a suffering WITH the Lord. He leads us to that place and through that place. He is manifesting greater glory through us, so that the work of the Holy Spirit has a fuller, more complete effect within this new nature, and so that the mind of the new creation is actively participating with Him.

"Yes, and all who desire to live godly in Christ Jesus will suffer persecution" (2 Timothy 3:12 NKJV). All kinds of suffering are true to every believer; the when, where, and how is not even a question for us. We bear our own unique cross. The end result is perfected by the wisdom we have received from what was purified in and through us during the process. The table is always set in the midst of our enemies. We will delight in Him, even if it is through the valley of the shadow of death. With the suffering there is always more glory. What do I mean by this? It means we have unique understanding in the spiritual realm that necessitates victory much more quickly, not only in our own lives but especially in the lives of others. We are a priceless jewel in His kingdom who bring many riches to countless others because of that transition from suffering to glory.

One time I had been mediating on all the answers to prayer concerning other people's lives. What came up in my spirit was a revelation of how almost every one of the people I had prayed for, who received complete turn-arounds to impossible situations, had not once taken time to thank me for praying for them. It wasn't that I was looking for any thankfulness from all those whom the Father had blessed, but I was deeply aware that these were my observations. This was the conversation that I had with the Father:

"I'm not going to pray for anyone anymore."

He answered my statement, "I want you to pray."

"Ok, I will pray, but I am not happy that they are not even thankful."

He replied, "I'm not happy about it either!"

All I could do was laugh. He needed me to see how He sees things, and I needed to have Him relate to me to see how I was seeing things too. We have such a wonderful, loving Heavenly Father. The burden from carrying all of that was lifted off of me immediately and completely. It still amuses me the way He had responded to the frustrated condition of my heart with, "*I'm not happy about it either!*"

Whatever the condition is that is not of the Father will respond to your spoken words because it does not align with His purposes. When you are *in Christ* with the *mind* of Christ you measure conditions by that which you consider

227

acceptable. By agreement in prayer, you connect with Him, releasing His glory. Any suffering is simple to understand by discerning from His perspective; it is anything that does not line up with what He declared. We have these highly skilled instruments: eyes and ears, to determine what is not good, not acceptable, and not perfect. These three areas will determine accurately how well we come into alignment with His thinking; therefore, we know exactly what to say and do in any given condition.

This condition within the body of Christ—being one—is the very purpose that Jesus died on the cross. Without us being *one* because of His glory, then there is no proof text able to convince us that Jesus has even been sent by the Father, although on a surface level we know He has been sent. But when we are *one* in Christ, therefore in the Father, we have greater expectancy. We know that the Father's glory, which has been deposited within us, will manifest through us as a witness that Jesus has been sent, and that He has accomplished all that the Bible says He did for us.

For I have given to them the words which You have given Me; and they have received them, and have known surely that I came forth from You; and they have believed that You sent Me. As You sent Me into the world, I also have sent them into the world. I in them, and You in Me; that they may be made perfect in one, and that the world may know that You have sent Me, and have loved them as You have loved Me. (John 17:8,18, 23 NKJV)

Excel in all that you do and say today and in the power of His might, which so powerfully works in you. Put into practice this wisdom, knowing that it is His glory that has been deposited in you. You only need to continually activate His glory through each and every condition set before you as an act of love on your part to honor Him with your life. Your words and your actions are what release His glory. You are giving birth to this heavenly substance each moment of your day. The wisdom of the Father has been that you would experience what Jesus has always experienced. It is His greatest treasure to pour out the riches of His glory, so that you would willingly walk with Him in all these wonderful works that manifest His most precious gift.

Riches of Glory

29

Bee Perfect

*T*he uniqueness of His glory is that it is only the Father's wisdom in the entire universe that creates as ONE. Everything else is a far cry from making one. Knowing this, opens the way for all things to be restored to Him, and it glorifies the Father because we become One in every area that He sets before us. Not through our own efforts, but through the revelation of the Holy Spirit, wisdom is perfected in those areas.

Here is the key to accurately catch this revelation: The glory that Jesus had with the Father from the beginning of creation is the same glory He deposited in us. It is the glory that created all there is. The glory is the treasure He purchased for us. What He bought and deposited within us when we became new creations is the wisdom and knowledge of His glory. Every time we taste His glory we understand something of the value of what He placed on our lives, which is the royal privilege of working with Him from the Throne of Glory.

That which He has placed within us makes the world grow strangely dim. Our desire for Him makes us fit for His kingdom. The leading of the Holy Spirit takes our fitness and makes us useful to Him now in this present world. We possess such a precious gift, a tremendous power, and a royal privilege to walk as sons and daughters, operating in the spiritual realm while we are still present in this physical world. What we possess, we have to give and impart to others. Our ability to impart His life to others is being tempered by the Holy Spirit.

The glory knowledge is royal language. This emphasize in our spirit is something He is doing. We have been given this royal privilege to have such an intimate relationship with the Father. He has entrusted us with the wisdom that has come from the Throne of Glory. Every word that the Holy Spirit speaks to us is this royal language, this royal wisdom. It is tremendous authority and honor that He has bestowed on us, His children. We have authority to wake up the rest of the body of Christ. Not unlike that prophet of old when asked, *Do these dry bones have life in them?* The Father is asking, because He has already promoted us, but we are about to be given our first assignment in this promotion and declare the royal words that the Holy Spirit speaks to our spirit! Amen!

One day, several years ago, my sisters and I were out playing in the field near the barn on the property where we lived. We happened to look up in the sky, and not quite ten feet above our heads a black cloud was hovering in the air. It was a swarm of honey bees, but there were thousands of them flying in such close proximity that you could not distinguish anything except this large dark mass suspended above us. We ran to the house and told our dad about them. Dressed only in a t-shirt and jeans, he went outside and into the barn to get one of several man-made beehives stored there. After placing the hive outside on a stand, he was able to spot and direct the queen bee into the hive (to separate this one queen bee from the colony of bees, an astonishing feat). Once the queen bee had entered that hive, the entire swarm suddenly and regimentally entered the hive as well. While they were in this swarming state, the bees were more docile and did not attack because they were relocating to their new home.

Many seasons after that first day when the bees settled into their new hive, my dad continued to collect the honey. Each time he would have to suit up because the bees, which were at one time docile, were now aggressive in protecting the hive from intruders. We were able to enjoy many pints and quarts of fresh honey from our honey bees. The queen bee is of course larger and fed the very same diet that all the other bees receive while they are still larvae. After about three days of this diet, the worker bees are no longer fed this *royal jelly*. It is this royal jelly that transforms the female worker bee into a larger egg-producing queen bee. The activated substance in this royal jelly is royalactin, a single protein that is designed by the Father to bring about these physiological changes. Royal jelly transforms the queen honey bee into possessing many differential characteristics than a regular honey bee, including anatomical proportions, longevity, and reproductive capacity. These changes occur from being fed large quantities of this royal jelly to a larva. This feeding is what ignites the changes at the molecular level for the development of a queen bee.

We can capture this thought quite easily when we understand that the Father is transforming our lives. He is transforming us into royalty. We are kings and priests in His kingdom. The Holy Spirit feeds us large quantities of *royal jelly*, the food that comes from the Throne of Glory. The changes made in us are in the depths at the spiritual level. *Man shall not live by bread alone, but by every word that comes from the Father*, now has greater meaning and purpose. We know that every word the Holy Spirit speaks to us is creatively transforming our entire being. He brings us up higher in thought, in purpose, and in the activities that are being manifested through us. Jesus clarified this by saying, *either believe the words I speak or the works I do*. "Do you not believe that I am in the Father, and the Father in Me? The words that I speak to you I do not speak on My own *authority*; but the Father who dwells in Me does the works. Believe Me that I am in the Father and the Father in Me, or else believe Me for the sake of the works themselves" (John 14:10, 11 NKJV).

There is something you want; there is something Jesus wants. He has provided all that you will ever need by giving you the same glory He had with the Father. Your favor is that He has granted you direct access to His glory which is being manifested through every revelation by the Holy Spirit. These kingdom secrets are being revealed by this knowledge of the glory. It should be noted that He wants to give more than we are ready to receive. That first level of understanding on how to operate with Him in His glory comes through the wisdom found in Scripture which the Holy Spirit made known to you. The Holy Spirit is following the very pattern that Jesus spoke concerning the secrets of the Kingdom. He declared that nothing is hidden that shall not be revealed. We grow from glory to glory by revelation. When the wisdom and revelation become our experiences then the knowledge of the glory is permanent residency. It is this intimate relationship that the Father decided we would enjoy all along.

The glimpses from Scripture are as training modules by the Holy Spirit to teach us His ways, His truth, and His life. They are specifically prepared by our Private Tutor, the Holy Spirit, to give unique lessons to each of us. We are given the opportunity to grow and perfect every revelation given so that the end result for anyone is that we know how to listen to and follow the voice of the Holy Spirit, and we understand how to work with Him in His glory. The two become one.

Consider the story of the wedding in Cana. Jesus displayed His first miracle, His first sign as the glory had been manifested through a Man. Whenever His glory is manifested many things shift in the spirit realm. In this case many believed in Jesus. The awakening of His glory is what manifested. The reality before was only words and ideas, but the manifestation of His glory solidified all things true in the spiritual realm. Mary said that they ran out of wine. The implication is a request to have more wine for the remaining days of the feast, which would have been a week long. This was only the third day of the feast. That fact alone is also a prophetic truth concerning the complete plan of the Father. Every detail when understood through the Father's eyes is an insight into all things He is doing. Jesus said many times that He only did what He saw the Father doing, and He only said what He heard the Father saying.

Jesus replied to His mother, "Woman, what does your concern have to do with Me? My hour has not yet come." This question and statement reveal the heart of the Father. There is something that the Father wants, there is something that we want, and like Mary, there is something we want with the immediate concerns all around us. The Father has His eyes on eternity, hence the words, "...My time has not yet come." Every covenant has two parts: our part, and (in this case) that which is the Father's part. The language for covenant is revealed by both. This would not be unlike any algebraic equation where there are unseemly parts on one side of the equation that do not necessarily resemble the other side. The equal sign by definition makes the two sides equal. This could become missed in the language of Mary and of Jesus, because from our perspective there is no way the water should have turned to wine.

Our simple answer many times is too shallow to give greater clarity as to what just happened. It is also the main reason we do not understand our own answers to prayer. It seems hit or miss most of the time as though it was only a faith accident, but we have no way of understanding the network of how things manifested. That is the great revelation of this knowledge of the glory—it reveals all things.

That which was hidden is now being revealed. This is a present tense experience in His glory. The Father's grand purpose for the church is that we would come up higher, operating in the heavenly realms and exercising authority over all the principalities and powers.

Mary's request for more wine and her statement, "Whatever He says to you, do it," make up the language of covenant: What she says and what Jesus says. The two become one—glory is manifested. Jesus did not ask the Father anything. It is not written that He gave thanks and the water transformed. He does not even touch the water Himself. Everything about this first miracle is a training module from the Holy Spirit on a greater scale to teach us on how to operate in the very same glory that He had deposited in us. Jesus said to the servants, "Fill the water pots with water," and then, "Draw some out now, and take it to the master of the feast." He said nothing else. These words, coupled with what Mary said, are the very words that manifested His glory. If you accelerated ahead to chapter 15 of John's gospel, Jesus said these words for us, "No longer do I call you servants, for a servant does not know what his master is doing; but I have called you friends, for all things that I heard from My Father I have made known to you." By this, the language of heaven has been transferred to us *now* with these rich treasures: Whatever we ask and declare will be manifested. It will be done now according to what we say.

To abide in Jesus and to have His words abide in us, is the sovereign decision of the Father. It glorifies the Father when we declare His words; it glorifies Jesus when the Holy

Spirit declares to us the language of heaven. The same stream from the Throne of Glory began with the Father. All that the Father has, has been given to Jesus, and all that Jesus received is now being declared to us. This is the same stream coming from the Throne. Now it is our turn to declare all that the Holy Spirit declares to us. This proves that we are no longer His servants, but friends, and disciples who display the knowledge of the glory, and manifest much fruit in all that we declare. It glorifies the Father that we are walking in the same glory as Jesus' earth-walk, and that we are being transformed from one level of glory to the next.

30

Exodus and Explode

$\mathcal{U}$ se this glory knowledge by the practice of walking in it as you speak these *pearls*. You will be ignited, everything you say will be ignited, and those listening will be ignited. A practical application is to take charge within the realm that He has already assigned to you. Look within your specific realm and discover anything that is NOT acceptable to you. Knowing this first will reinforce how you will use His glory to turn the situation around. Map all of your thinking through this filter: *I consider this present suffering not worthy to be compared to the glory that is in me that is about to be revealed and released through my spoken words.* "For I consider that the sufferings of this present time are not worthy to be compared with the glory which shall be revealed in us" (Romans 8:18 NKJV).

Let's take a closer look at the actual meaning behind the phrase **shall be revealed** found in Romans 8:18. A very good friend of mine and a scholar in biblical Hebrew, Dr. Adrian Bernal, once researched the depths of this phrase.

The rich meaning he discovered in research, which had been hidden by the Holy Spirit, Dr. Bernal translated from the text written in the original Hebrew as, **exodus** and **explode**.[1] This was extremely eye-opening, since it had confirmed what I knew was true about His glory already. To follow this with some practical understanding, the Holy Spirit speaks to us fresh word, which then begins to radiate inside us and rise up until it *exodus* (exits) and *explodes* as it comes out of our mouths.

That is in complete agreement with what the Greek language expresses in principle in 2 Corinthians 4:4, "...lest the light should shine on them." It first *radiates* within us, and then it *beams forth* out of our mouths. The Holy Spirit fuses our words with His glory so that they are one. Tremendous power is being released in every word He has spoken to us, and then it is released through us with the same authority in which He delivered that word to our spirit.

---

[1] "To be about to" (μέλλω mĕllō, mel´-lo) is a strengthened form of the idea of expectation; meaning a very strong intention for something to be revealed. The Hebrew golah is to intend a strong sense of revelation.

Therefore, "about to be revealed" means with deep conviction of an expectation or a sense of the Spirit of God bursting (exploding) forth from within. Exodus (or exit) as you explain can be paired with it, but it has more to do with being exiled or leaving from exile, which does come from golah (revealed) but with a birthing of expectation like the children of Israel waiting for 400 years to be delivered. Therefore, the glory that is to be revealed is the bursting out from within the deep-desired expectations of God's glory that cannot be contained. Thus, with the next verse (Romans 8:19), all creation awaits for the children of God to burst forth with the glory that has been placed within by the desire and expectation of the birthing of the Holy Spirit.

Meditate and yield to only the voice of the Holy Spirit. Learn His voice above anything else you will ever develop with Him. "But you, beloved, building yourselves up on your most holy faith, praying in the Holy Spirit" (Jude 1:20 NKJV).

It comes to you by revelation that the glory is greater. Because it is greater, it does not matter what the condition is that is set before you. The glory will transform it effortlessly on your part. You just remain a willing vessel, yielded to the voice of the Holy Spirit. Be willing to speak His word. Your willingness proves you are His disciple, it manifests fruit, and it lets His glory flow through you. This glory flows from the Father from the Throne of Glory to Jesus. The Holy Spirit then takes the glory that belongs to Jesus and declares it to you. Finally, you speak in alignment with what the Holy Spirit speaks to you. Now Glory is being given to the Father which completes the heavenly model. Christ is in you and you are in Him, operating now with intimate experiences in Christ.

You look at what is set before you and decide that it does not even compare with His glory. You decide in your heart that now you know His glory is greater. You think differently. You already know that nothing is greater than this glory which is in you. You are being taught exactly how to manifest His glory each and every time you walk through any condition. His glory is capable of destroying every work of the enemy. It is up to us to be willing vessels and to work with the Holy Spirit as He teaches us to be effective in this physical realm. We must learn to lean on our ability to trust Him implicitly rather than leaning on our own strength and abilities. *Self* must be put aside completely; the spirit-man must rule. The power of resurrection is something the Apostle Paul had discovered. He learned to rely totally on the glory within him. He could declare, "I have been crucified with Christ; it is no longer I who live, but Christ lives in me; and the life which I now live in the flesh I live by faith in the Son of God, who loved me and gave Himself for me" (Galatians 2:20 NKJV).

A few years ago I was driving home in the mountains while it was still daylight. I came around a corner when a doe trotted across the road in front of me, a typical occurrence that happens quite often. Suddenly, a fawn came darting out of the woods and across the road to catch up with its mom. However, this little one was oblivious to my vehicle and ran straight into it. My SUV flipped the small deer around and it fell dead on the road behind me. I talked to Father God shortly afterwards, "Father God, forgive me. I did not run into this little deer on purpose. The fawn came running out and hit my vehicle. I am asking in the same way Jesus sent His word and healed the centurion's servant—that You fill my words with Your glory and resurrect the deer back to life." The fawn was resurrected back to life! Amazing! I remember, though, how effortless within me this experience felt. Expect supernatural transformation within you that receives pure glory wisdom.

When Jesus gave us insight as to why He came, "The thief does not come except to steal, and to kill, and to destroy. I have come that they may have life, and that they may have *it* more abundantly" (John 10:10 NKJV). The language that John used in the opening remarks of his gospel, "In Him was Life, and the Life was the light of men" (John 1:4) reveals that the Life that Jesus came to give is actually the glory—the light of men. The Life that Jesus declares we may have is two-fold: First, it is the light of life that becomes ignited. Second, it is the light that radiates and beams forth from us.

His revelation to us comes in at a certain level and resonates within; it brings our thinking up higher to where He thinks. When simple practical application is given to any opportunity, it becomes this, "Taste and see that the Lord is good." What we have tasted is His word abiding in our mouths, and we see the effect of His glory in the words that manifest (become visible). It totally *rearranges the furniture in us!* We know we did nothing; it was effortless on our part, except that we have intimately experienced His glory as it manifested through us. This is the same way His glory was being manifested through Jesus. Because of this our joy is piqued just as Jesus said it would be, "… and that your joy might be full!"

The following is a response from another believer regarding the previous paragraph, and it reveals the power and nature of how *the knowledge of the glory* truly makes us free—it rearranges our *furniture*:

Larry, this word is profound, with intricacies, a perfect fit to the encouragement of His Spirit. It lends itself to the momentum of the Spirit into (for me), uncharted waters— deep waters. Unconditional love is not something I know. The westernized church model is one of conditional

contradictions and performance orientation. Although I
have known this reality for more than a dozen years, like
hinds feet on high places, God is steadying my walk on
the narrowest path into what momentarily feels like
wilderness, but with liberty. It seems His plan and good
pleasure is once for all to escape its clutches—its
corporate model of top-down hierarchal standards—its
reengineered interpretation of Scripture as applied to
church life (which is not in fact, life-giving). No more
jumping through hoops for acceptance. His sufficiency is,
by His measure, beyond measure. And His provision in all
things shall be seen, unconditionally, free of the broken,
ever draining man-made (manufactured) system. For me,
this is my exodus—no more brick making.
–Author Unknown

When the fingers of man are in anything, the signature
and authenticity that only comes from the Father is lacking. I
am a firm believer that following the voice of the Holy Spirit—
obedience to the faith—is everything. It is His fine-tuning that
perfects us anyway, not things done in our own strength.
This is why the wisdom, revelation, and knowledge of the
glory of the Lord are vital, because it is the actual work of
what the Holy Spirit does within us. He sets us apart for this
personalized tutoring that is specifically designed for each of
us. It is this revelation lifestyle that coincides with what Jesus
said, "Man shall not live by bread alone, but by every word
that proceeds from the mouth of God."

Jesus reveals what the Holy Spirit is feeding us in John 16, "I still have many things to say to you, but you cannot bear them now. However, when He, the Spirit of truth, has come, He will guide you into all truth; for He will not speak on His own authority, but whatever He hears He will speak; and He will tell you things to come. He will glorify Me, for He will take of what is Mine and declare it to you. All things that the Father has are Mine. Therefore I said that He will take of Mine and declare it to you" (John 16:12-15 NKJV). Every word that comes from the Father is being revealed from the Throne of Glory; therefore, consider that every word the Holy Spirit declares to us is *glory knowledge*. Hence, the phrase, **"the knowledge of the glory"** found both in the Old Covenant and the New Covenant, Habakkuk 2:14 and 2 Corinthians 4:6, respectively.

The Holy Spirit is revealing to us the very realms, domains, and spheres that we truly do operate in with His glory. He has sovereignly appointed to us these jurisdictions in which we command, so that what we speak, remains. This knowledge totally rearranges the *furniture* and establishes His kingdom, effortlessly on our part. All that the Holy Spirit speaks is filled with both the wisdom and the power of His glory. Christ is the wisdom and the power of God. That one word, *Christ*, which manifests in us and through us, came from the Throne of Glory. The revelation ignites us when received as it engrafts to our souls. It rearranges our thinking, transforms our will, and is expressed passionately through our emotions. We have total confidence in Him. Christ is our healer. That statement contains both the wisdom and the power to overcome anything set before us.

Riches of Glory

31

The Litmus Test

his heavenly substance—His glory—bonds together willingly in everything, for it transforms the conditions so that it glorifies the Father. "But all things that are exposed are made manifest by the light, for whatever makes manifest is light" (Ephesians 5:13 NKJV). His glory makes and holds everything together; it becomes ONE in Him and is the foundation of all things. Thoughts that repel His glory have not been subjected to Christ.

You can do your own litmus test, by testing the waters with morsels from the knowledge of the glory. It will reveal the true heart conditions and those whom He is calling closer to Himself. Jesus said in John 12:32 that if He is lifted up, all men will be drawn to Him. He is the Lord of glory, and lifting up this knowledge and the person of Christ in us is what draws all men. Light transforms the conditions; even total darkness becomes light.

This exposure to the light is the characteristic of His glory in us. We walk in the light. We walk into any place bringing this light. Without saying a word, it is igniting others in the same place, whether they believe or not. Another revelation by the Father as revealed by the Holy Spirit is that the Father has complete and total authority. He orders our steps even when we are unaware He is doing so. Nothing manifests around us from the kingdom of darkness unless the Father has authorized it. If He has authorized it, then He has also appointed us to manifest His glory. He has lovingly chosen that we are graciously prepared to bear this because of the training He has already provided. He is just giving us an opportunity to experience His glory through any outside pressure from the enemy that He opens to us.

You release His glory with your words that have become fused with His glory. It is His glory that will transform every realm that He has assigned to you. The adverse conditions that oppose what you know to be true concerning Him are subject to change because of the glory He deposited within you. You can tell the glory is being released when you experience peace in the midst of the trials and every other kind of pressure. Not just the peace within, but peace that is radiating out of you in ways that engage others. You did nothing but show up.

When we pray in the spirit, we are truly building ourselves up in the highest level of faith that we can experience. The ability to stay focused is a serendipity effect of our faith being built up. We have perfect peace because of that level of engagement with being in His presence. We were supercharged by His presence. Jesus never has any shortfall staying focused, nor is He confused about what to do in any area of life. All of the qualities that He is, we are as well, for Christ is in us. His glory begins to be released in us through the flow of His Spirit in all that we say and do. Jesus said, "Be perfect as Your Heavenly Father is perfect," and this is the reality that manifests in His glory. All things begin to fit together perfectly from what the Holy Spirit reveals.

He has given us tools, so that we can measure accurately and prove where to manifest His glory through us. If something is not good, nor acceptable, nor perfect then it is not God's will. Therefore, His glory in is, which is about to be revealed and released through our spoken words in spite of the darkness before us, transforms the condition to that which is good, acceptable, and perfect. In fact, those conditions are ordered as *lab experiments* for His glory to be manifested through us. This wisdom is the private tutoring of the Holy Spirit to bring us into alignment to think as the Father is thinking.

It is a matter of truly learning to yield to Him in obedience to His voice. The Scripture calls this, *obedience to the faith.* The faith is to know His voice and to follow Him accurately which aligns us with the Father. This is how Jesus walked. He only said what He heard the Father saying, and He only did what He saw the Father doing. Yet, He declares in prayer, "Father I sanctify Myself." I thought He was already sanctified! He is, but the ingredients that go into the Bread of Life recipe are the same that show up in us. Now we have a more accurate understanding of our new nature, so we don't try to improve our walk which is just patching up the old nature through the old nature's pride. Any improvements that we do on our own may satisfy our thinking, but it is certainly not surrendered to the Holy Spirit's private tutoring lessons.

Anything that is taking place in the physical realm that is not acceptable is a result of us not taking care of things in the spiritual realm first. What the Holy Spirit speaks to us by this word is the fine-tuning that takes place within us. This appropriates our faith in ways that effortlessly release His glory through us. The eyes and ears of those who operate in His glory are highly developed instruments. By them we measure things around us with the filtering of His word. Jesus said it this way, "Take heed what you hear. With the same measure you use, it will be measured to you" (Mark 4:24 NKJV).

Let me say this again, anything that manifests in the physical realm is something that has not been taken care of in the spiritual realm. He has given us His glory to take care of matters that are set before us. It does not matter what the condition is. It does matter, though, that we understand that what we declare in the spiritual realm is the reality that we experience. The obvious results of what we see and hear are equivalent to the level of spiritual maturity that has been expressed in any particular realm.

"His intent was that now, through the church, the manifold wisdom of God should be made known to the rulers and authorities in the heavenly realms" (Ephesians 3:10 NIV).

If we sense and know chaos is in the realm He has assigned to us, then in the spirit we have not released peace. The greater ONE is in us, so that we can accurately discern what is dominating the realm to which we are assigned. Act on His behalf and expect the condition to transform in this way; whatever is true in heaven is also true in this earth realm.

Jesus had been led into the wilderness by the Holy Spirit, and it was there where He encountered the enemy (the tempter, according to some Bible versions). We understand this direct encounter with the enemy from the accounts found in chapters four of both Matthew and Luke. It should be clearly understood that Jesus is fully God and fully Man. The genius and wisdom of the Father as He is manifested in Jesus, "The Father is in Me and I am in the Father," absolutely takes the Holy Spirit in us to unveil this powerful revelation. Jesus was hungry in the wilderness and thirsty on the cross. He was asleep in the bow of the boat, and prayed until droplets of blood ran down His face. Nevertheless, the Father's wisdom and power were displayed in the moment of Jesus' temptation. When His flesh would have screamed the loudest, the Holy Spirit in Him subdued the human nature as Jesus proclaimed the Word.

Then Jesus was led up by the Spirit into the wilderness to be tempted by the devil. And when He had fasted forty days and forty nights, afterward He was hungry. Now when the tempter came to Him, he said, 'If You are the Son of God, command that these stones become bread.' But He answered and said, "It is written, 'Man shall not live by bread alone, but by every word that proceeds from the mouth of God.'" (Matthew 4:1-4 NKJV)

Our flesh does cry out when we are experiencing any difficulty or circumstance; it longs for the *least* amount of suffering. We seek the comfort of others, so that perhaps they could carry some of the burden that weighs heavily upon us. While it is good to have the comfort of one's friend, our first response should always be to seek the Lord Jesus Christ. It is for these purposes that He sent the Holy Spirit, to comfort us in those times. Remember that Christ has become to us both the power and the wisdom of God. Accessing His power in the midst of any trial is where wisdom needs to become our comfort food.

I have both a word and revelation given to me by the Holy Spirit that I believe we can incorporate into our experiences so that we are raised up from the dust and placed on the Throne of Glory. "He raises the poor from the dust and lifts the beggar from the ash heap, to set them among princes and make them inherit the throne of glory" (1 Samuel 2:8 NKJV). That word is *pressure*. There are many places in our lives where we experience some kind of pressure from the kingdom of darkness. It is generally nothing specific, but feels more like a constant pressure that is just as real all the same. A Bible word that compares to the word *pressure* is *affliction*. In our conversations today, we may hear it this way, "You don't know what I am going through. I am under a lot of pressure!" It is elusive; though it affects the way we think and act.

The accompanying revelation from the Holy Spirit dealing with this pressure from the enemy is this;

Push back with His promises until peace is manifesting from you.

The pressure is a spiritual activity from the enemy that is aimed at squelching something we are doing with the Holy Spirit. The enemy does not have any authority now over the believer, but he can apply pressure. It's a deception. I will repeat that revelation from the Holy Spirit again. You can engage that invisible constant pressure as something that needs to be dealt with. It does not overwhelm because you know that you can take any one of those precious promises depending on your specific need and use it to press against the pressure from the enemy until peace is manifesting from you. This is how you resist the enemy with results that can be measured, even before you see complete changes. You are enjoying peace.

Push back with His promises until peace is manifesting from you.

Riches of Glory

32

The Finger of God

The enemy has always challenged the Glory in one way or another. Either by challenging the words, revelation, wisdom of the Father, and the leading of the Holy Spirit in order to usurp the authority from the Throne of Glory; or by challenging the works (signs, miracles, and wonders) by placing false honor on everything and anyone besides the Father of Glory. The enemy is still a thief, and comes only to steal, kill, and destroy; he will do anything to keep us from understanding this good news of the Glory. The enemy is also extremely jealous and filled with pride over the delight that the Father has displayed toward us when He gave us tremendous power and authority. The Heavenly Father has placed His richest treasure in vessels of clay to manifest this great power that surpasses all we could ever be, hope for, or imagine. "We now have this light shining in our hearts, but we ourselves are like fragile clay jars containing this great treasure. This makes it clear that our great power is from God, not from ourselves" (2 Corinthians 4:7 NLT).

Jesus walked as an Old Covenant Man filled with the Holy Spirit. We walk as a New Covenant man filled with the Holy Spirit. The language of this New Covenant is the very nature and core of who we are. We have Christ in the old nature going to the cross, forever fulfilling the Old Covenant. We also have Christ rising from the dead, forever fulfilling the New Covenant. The glory of the Father raised Jesus from the dead. The glory raises us to a whole new way of living, effortlessly on our part, as we are yielded to the voice of the Holy Spirit. We are in Christ seated in the heavenlies now. He empowered us as ministers of this New Covenant—a ministry to restore all things. We are seated with Him now, empowered with His glory activated through us.

Jesus said to His disciples, "Have the faith of God". Use your imagination for a minute and picture Jesus holding out His hand with an opened palm up saying, "Have the faith of God." That faith was imparted to them when He spoke. Dear friends, we already have faith, but what we do not have yet is faith in our mouths. As the Apostle Paul said in Romans 10:18, "The word is near you, in your mouth and in your heart." When it is only in our heart, we believe alright, but nothing has taken place outwardly until we speak and declare His words.

When Jesus spoke to the fig tree, His disciples were amazed the next day to see it withered up from the roots and dead. Picture again Jesus reaching toward them with the palm of His hand saying, "Have the faith of God." Each of us have been given a measure of faith. It is a gift. There is faith in God's word because He is a faith God. All things that He is, the Word is also. It is so important to receive the engrafted word in our souls, so that it will manifest according to its kind. If understood clearly, every word from the Father feeds our spirit-man, which was dead before, but is alive now in Christ. All life came into being because of Christ.

It should be just as amazing to us as it was for the disciples when they saw the fig tree after Jesus had cursed it by speaking to it, "Let no one eat fruit from you ever again!" The following truth should resonate within us: Jesus, the Tree of Life prophetically declared that *we would never eat from the other tree in the garden ever again.* Jesus is the vine, and we are grafted into Him as the branches; His glory is the life that flows through us. We are given faith as a gift, for He said, "Have the faith of God." The fig tree illustration (albeit a negative connotation) is one example of how we receive from Jesus when He speaks to us for our good. The effects are immediate and permanent. His word is imparted to us, for it is life to us from Him.

Jesus summed it up by saying, "These things I have spoken to you, that My joy may remain in you, and that your joy may be full" (John 15:11 NKJV). When He speaks, joy is being imparted to you; it is contagious and fills your entire being. Peter gives more insight on this, "...joy unspeakable and full of glory." When His glory is activated you have joy unspeakable and overflowing. Joy is an indicator within you that glory is rising up and out of you. The next circumstance that you shall face should be an opportunity to rejoice, no matter what degree of difficulty. With the presence of joy, you know glory is being revealed and released through your spoken words. Jesus said that our joy would be full. When we speak we taste what joy tastes like, and we get to see the fruit (results) with our own eyes. "Oh, taste and see that the Lord is good; blessed is the man who trusts in Him!" (Psalm 34:8 NKJV).

Every word from the Father is coming from the Throne of Glory, so that every Rhema by the Holy Spirit truly is *glory knowledge* (intimate experiential knowledge). Scripture calls it "the knowledge of the glory." This phrase is found word for word in both in the Old Covenant (Habakkuk 2:14) and the New Covenant (2 Corinthians 4:6). In the New Covenant there is rich insight to be received from what is written. The Father commanded *light* to shine in us, but it does not become initially activated until Christ is in us, which is only in seed form. His faith which is also in seed form in our heart begins to produce the first evidence when it is in our mouths. We must be in Christ to complete this heavenly model, to transform the condition from only *hope* of glory, to Christ the Lord of glory. This is Bible hope—total expectation of what has been believed.

We are told that Jesus is in us when we first believe, but truthfully, we have not yet stepped into His life. That *glory seed* is in us, true, but it has not yet been activated to the point that it radiates within, rises up, and beams forth from us. That is why Colossians 1:27 states, "...Christ in us the HOPE of glory." The glory has not yet been awakened or activated; it is hope. I have a very good example for how the Holy Spirit revealed this to me. Let's say you were out on a date with your gentleman friend (speaking to the ladies).

He brings you back to your place. You are looking at him, he is looking at you, and chemistry is in the air. He reaches into his pocket to offer you a card that says *a hope of a kiss*. Do you want the card or do you want the kiss? Until His word, which is one with His glory, is on our lips, the relationship lacks that vibrant spark that awakens His glory in us. The enemy had been very effective at deceiving the body of Christ, keeping us blind to this good news concerning His glory, but not any longer. Now we know!

Several of my friends and I were visiting the home of a family of believers one evening. We were encouraging one another with His word and exchanging stories that the Lord had walked us through. The mother of this particular family had been a believer ever since she was a child. The grandmother was also a very strong believer. I truly believe that a spiritual pedigree is imparted when we deliberately decide to impart the wisdom, revelation, and intimate experiences in Christ with our children, including those whom He brings across our path. The Father orders the steps of the righteous, not just in the way that we walk, but every detail of our lives. We catch the revelation from what opens before us and then we understand the significance of how the Father orders our steps.

The mother began sharing with us a particular experience that she had while she was still in grade school. At the school she attended, there were a few older children who would meet behind the school buildings. They were practicing a form of spiritual darkness in an attempt to invoke some kind of power to levitate a table. Apparently, they were getting results. (The kingdom of darkness does counterfeit works with false signs, wonders, and miracles.) She continued with her story about how many other children, who were fascinated by what they saw and heard, tried to get her to come around to the backside of the school playgrounds. She just kept refusing, knowing that it did not sit right within her own spirit.

When she went home to talk to her mom about these particular events, her mom directly told her, "Well, you know that if this is not God, then it is another spirit. Because you are a believer and a child of God, you can just put your hand on the table and it will not rise at all. Greater is He who is in you, than he that is in the world." The little girl went to school the very next day filled with faith from the words her mother had shared with her. When the other children asked her again to come to the backside of the school, she went. As before, all of them who had gathered started to engage what they had done previously. The little girl, empowered by the words of the Spirit given to her from her mom, reached only a finger out to touch the table. All those present were taken completely by surprise. The glory of God subdued this dark manifestation from being able to produce anything. The little girl was the useful vessel to manifest His glory. The children quickly dispersed and never gathered together again to naively practice what had been revealed as the devil's works. It was no match whatsoever for the glory of God.

33

Can a Nation Be Born in a Day?

$\mathcal{Q}$ uestions may arise that this may be all well and good about these truths concerning His glory or as the title of this book indicates, *"Riches of Glory"*, but what about where we live now? What about the things that are happening in our world on a daily basis? What can we do to change the effects that we see as a rapid decay all around us? Didn't Jesus prophesy that all these things would take place? Is there anything that we could do to thwart this in our own lives?

The Holy Spirit has revealed to us that *all authority in heaven and earth* have been given to Jesus. This authority has been given to us, but the wisdom of operating in that authority has not been completely understood as yet. We have the ability to practice working with the Holy Spirit's leading in our lives in order to engage this authority. We can prove the Spirit's wisdom is being conveyed to us by the Heavenly Father. He does not allow anything to manifest around us in which He has not personally developed and trained us already to walk.

You may recall the story of Jonah, how he was told to go preach the word to Ninevah. Jonah was not completely yielded to that idea of going to the city; however, God had already called and appointed him for this very specific task. We know the results: Jonah preached to the city. Their impending doom quickly arrested their attention and the whole city repented. The whole city was changed in a day. Some biblical scholars have indicated that at the time of Jonah, the population of Ninevah was anywhere from 150,000 to 600,000 people. The working of the Spirit through the prophet Jonah took place under the Old Covenant. We have a better covenant and better promises, operating with greater glory.

Jonah was in the belly of the whale for three days and three nights. This is exactly what Jesus declared about Himself, "For as Jonah was three days and three nights in the belly of the great fish, so will the Son of Man be three days and three nights in the heart of the earth" (Matthew 12:40 NKJV). However, we know that the glory of the Father raised Jesus from the grave. The significance of this comparison might get missed if we don't understand this shadow or type, which was the same glory that raised Jonah out of the fish as well. Jesus was crowned with glory after being raised from the dead. One of the manifestations of the glory that we can recognize from Jonah is that the whole city was transformed in a day by the glory of the Father. What is true with Jonah is also true with Jesus. Can a nation be born in a day? We have more evidence now, knowing what glory was manifested through Jonah after being in the belly of the fish. The glory that is manifested through the body of Christ, being greater, *can* transform a nation in a day. Do you believe this?

The Holy Spirit will place us in specific realms where we begin experiencing greater authority than we have ever known before, just from acting on His wisdom concerning His glory. You will note that Jesus is the Tree of Life and spoke these words *either believe the words that I say or believe the works I do.* Two branches spring up from the Tree of Life: Words and Works. You will be able to track this in your own thinking by understanding that this is how the Father was described in Isaiah—His thoughts and His ways. And again the comparison of Christ in the way He is manifested by what is written, "...Christ the power of God and the wisdom of God" (1 Corinthians 1:24 NKJV).

What insightful revelation do we get from Jesus when He declared the kind of conditions we would see in the last days? Most of the time it is assumed that because Jesus spoke prophetically about what would take place in these last days that there is nothing we can do about it. If you will allow this image to capture your imagination, Jesus stated clearly what He was picking up on His *radar screen.* No matter how many images that He was seeing on the horizon of that *radar screen,* He is still the Lord of glory having all authority in heaven and earth. It does not mean that the Captain of your ship cannot do anything about the enemy. This is the Father's desire and protection to prepare us in advance, so that we have total confidence in His word and in His glory within us.

We should have a much higher understanding of the Father's ways than the prophet from old in Nineveh. Jonah was being fine-tuned by the Father to declare His word. He was also aware of the tremendous effect that the word would have on all those citizens of that ancient city. Now with the words of Jesus in our mouth, the wisdom of the Father, and the Spirit's leading, we should expect greater works than this Old Covenant prophet. Our imaginations should be totally set free to come into alignment with the Father's wisdom, "Can a nation be born in a day?"

You are strictly His and have been bought with a price: the blood that was shed to pay a price that could not have been paid by any other. Jesus willingly became your substitute. He prayed for you directly, so that you have received this wisdom of His glory restored now for all generations. This word which is the very life of Christ filling your soul has first become quickened by the Holy Spirit within your own spirit. You received a new nature, a new spirit, and also the Holy Spirit when you called on that Name. The Name of Jesus has power above all other names; it gives you authority and power to become a child of the living God.

The Father of glory empowered you with His life, the very life of His glory. Now through you His glory is awakening throughout the entire body of Christ. In the same way that Christ had been raised from the dead by the glory of the Father, you too, are being raised up to your rightful place in His kingdom. You were asleep; you were not yet activated and empowered by His living word. One word from the

Father of glory gave you life. *"In Him was life, and the life was the light of men"* (John 1:4 NKJV).

Without Him we have no life. His glory is our life, and it is permeated through every cell of our being. It is His word which was spoken that made us new creations in Christ. We have entered into a whole new realm that was never available to us before. The Father Himself has qualified us and translated us into this Kingdom of Light. As His ambassadors, we show forth the marvelous works of His glory through everything that we say and do, yielded to the Holy Spirit completely. "But you are a chosen generation, a royal priesthood, a holy nation, His own special people, that you may proclaim the praises of Him who called you out of darkness into His marvelous light; who once were not a people but are now the people of God, who had not obtained mercy but now have obtained mercy" (I Peter 2:9,10 NKJV).

Meditate on the combined truth in relationship with Him, so that it resonates within you who have already been bought: "Without Him I can do nothing" and "With Him nothing shall be impossible". Jesus gave the most precise and clear revelation to how the glory of the Father was operating so very intimately through and in Him. "Do you not believe that I am in the Father, and the Father in Me? The words that I speak to you I do not speak on My own authority; but the Father who dwells in Me does the works" (John 14:10 NKJV). This revelation has been imparted to us as well, "If you abide in Me, and My words abide in you, you will ask what you desire, and it shall be done for you. By this My Father is glorified, that you bear much fruit; so you will be My disciples" (John 15:7, 8 NKJV).

Any level of faith exercised and received in one area, such as you get your health back, works within you to know and believe the reality that His glory overcame in that area. You can then stretch your imagination around more promises from the Father. It might get expressed that you can get your family back, or you can get your community back. Watch out! It might get contagious and you may imagine that you can get your country back. Of course, we know His plan is bigger than that, but why interfere with young ones beginning to step out in faith and learning how to stand by grace on any one promise. We should be so saturated in His love that any act of expressing His love to His dear ones means that we come alongside them, believing for the impossible as well. That language of impossible is only an opportunity for His glory to manifest. His glory, which is greater than all, will be a joy for everyone when they taste and see how good the Lord truly is. We thank you Father that You have lovingly chosen that every suffering the world around us faces is an excellent opportunity for the demonstration of Your Holy Spirit to reveal Your love and power. In this way, all whom You draw to Yourself, have their faith rested on Your majesty and power, and not human wisdom. In Jesus' mighty name, Amen!

This day I am in agreement with you. The Father has deposited His glory within you. All that He has given to you is already within you: every treasure, all the power, and all the health is already there within you. It now needs only to be activated to see the manifestation of it with your physical eyes. Before we see evidence with our physical eyes, we must see the living reality with our spiritual eyes, which is everything that we need. It is already available in His glory, which is in us. So we can begin rejoicing now that you already have total healing. You already have all your finances restored, etc.

One word from the Holy Spirit will activate and access this glory within you. One word from Jesus, and Peter was walking on water. The outward symptoms are only that a temporary condition currently training you so that a demand is placed on the storehouse of riches within you, which in turn rises up from you through your spoken words. In truth, every adverse condition is an opportunity to place a demand on you to manifest His glory from within. Our minds are not developed as yet to be proactive in His glory, but as it is, they are mostly just reactive to the conditions around us. Absolutely be assured of this, His glory, which is in you and is much greater than what anyone is presently facing, is about to be revealed and released.

A couple of developmental activities in the spiritual realm that must be exercised more are: praying in the spirit much and taking communion much. By praying in the spirit much, your faith is built up to the highest level and the most holy perfection within you. By taking communion much you have simply entered that supernatural realm to believe and imagine for anything possible by saying with your own mouth while taking communion, "Without Christ I can do nothing. With Christ nothing is impossible."

I thank you Father for rejoicing over me, long before I ever knew You. I thank you Father for Your favor. I thank you Father for Your wisdom. I ask You now to flood my spirit with the wisdom, revelation, and knowledge of Your glory. I totally thank you that in all You have done, You did so by giving to me Your glory. I thank you Father that You have qualified me to have direct access to Your glory. I thank you Father that every pain and lack must cease now in Jesus' name. I thank you for the peace that radiates out of me, assuring me that everything I ask for is the evidence that Your glory is being activated within; and rising up, rising up, and radiating out from me. Once activated, the glory rises up and radiates from me bringing an overwhelming peace throughout the entire realm to which You have appointed me. I thank you Father that this peace is destroying the works of the enemy within the entire realm to which You appointed to me. I am rejoicing now that You delight in not only setting me completely free, but also everyone who has walked into my realm is being transformed by Your glory. Thank you Father for such an amazing gift by Your precious promises that Your Holy Spirit teaches me to give, out of the abundance of Your glory that is flowing freely within me. Holy Father it is awesome being Your child. Amen!

STREAMS OF GLORY
ministries

MISSION STATEMENT

Our ministry is to train up the body of Christ in the knowledge of the Glory, by activating them into the ministry which they have received, and empowering them to take this vision to the ends of the earth.

We emphasize discipleship with the gifts of the Spirit; more specifically, a prophetic message, which ushers in the return of Christ for His bride – the glorious church. Furthermore, stretching our imaginations to move in the miraculous and supernatural as simple as breathing.

Get Involved with Streams of Glory!

• **Email:** timebytez@me.com
• **Call:** 307-413-2894
• **OR copy this page, fill out and mail to address below:**

Father God, You have qualified and empowered me to:

❏ **Pray** for Streams Of Glory Ministries
❏ **Host/Volunteer** Purity & Power Conference in my area
❏ **Partner** with Streams Of Glory Ministries

In Jesus' name, Amen!

_____
name

_____
address

_____
city / state / zip

_____
email

Mail form to:
PO Box 12
Tahoe City, CA
96145

OTHER BOOKS BY THE AUTHOR

Larry Thompson grew up in a time when you still walked to school, just eclipsing that time previous, when you walked in five feet of snow, uphill both ways. You still had to get up from the couch to change the station on television, and adjust the connection by moving the rabbit ears (antenna, for those who have not heard of them). Most people remember very well the exact things that happened in traumatic times, such as the day Kennedy was shot, or, recently, 9/11. What Larry Thompson has taken time to remind us of, is that the simple ways produce the richest experiences. He became a born-again believer shortly after graduating from high school, more than forty years ago, and has since been successfully discipling others. He entered the U.S. Navy, achieving the Academic Award right out of basic training.

Once, while living in Massachusetts, he was given the opportunity to act as an assistant to a local high school football team. The coach, after losing a football game with a large deficit in the score, asked Larry, if he (the coach) could have done anything differently. Larry's reply to the coach was one of those encouraging words that has been one of his life signatures—to speak into another person's soul. The coach gave Larry a big bear hug, totally affected by his words. The words in Larry Thompson's most recent book, from this aggressive book series project, are aimed at your life becoming greatly encouraged as well. In his words, "This journey of being taught to follow intimately the voice of the Holy Spirit concerning His glory ignites everything within the believer's life, and you will never be the same. You will no longer have faith accidents, but real depth and understanding in that spiritual realm—the Glory."

Secrets of the Kingdom Series

Glory Revealed
ISBN: 978-1628712971

The Gospel of the Glory
ISBN: 978-1727631531

Riches of Glory
ISBN: 978-1072098133

From Glory to Glory Series

Guardians of the Glory
Available as an eBook http://books.apple.com/us/book/id1236591748

Tanya,

Without Him we can do nothing,
With Him nothing is impossible

Blessings

Thompson

2-17-21

Made in the USA
Middletown, DE
28 January 2021